Handmade Gatherings

HANDMADE GATHERINGS

Recipes & Crafts for Seasonal
Celebrations & Potluck Parties

Ashley English

Photographs by Jen Altman

ROOST BOOKS
Boston & London 2014

Roost Books
An imprint of Shambhala Publications, Inc.
Horticultural Hall
300 Massachusetts Avenue
Boston, Massachusetts 02115
roostbooks.com

9 8 7 6 5 4 3 2 1

First Edition
Printed in the United States of America

⊗ This edition is printed on acid-free paper
that meets the American National Standards
Institute z39.48 Standard.
♲ Shambhala makes every effort to print on
recycled paper. For more information please
visit www.shambhala.com.

Distributed in the United States
by Penguin Random House LLC
and in Canada by Random House of Canada Ltd

Designed by Daniel Urban-Brown

LIBRARY OF CONGRESS
CATALOGING-IN-PUBLICATION DATA

English, Ashley, 1976–
Handmade gatherings: recipes and crafts for
seasonal celebrations and potluck parties /
Ashley English; photographs by Jen Altman.—
First edition.
Pages   cm
Includes bibliographical references and index.
ISBN 978-1-61180-056-2 (hardcover: alk. paper)
1. Seasonal cooking. 2. Handicraft.
3. Entertaining. I. Title.
TX714.E498 2014
641.5'64—dc23
2013005179

TO GLENN AND HUXLEY, MY PERENNIAL REASONS FOR CELEBRATING.

Contents

Introduction ix Gathering the Essentials xvii

SPRING

Spring to Life 3
Wild Things 21
The Good Egg 35
Pollinating Ideas 51

SUMMER

Like a Rolling Stone (Fruit) 67
Southern Comfort 83
Ice Cream Social 101
In a Pickle 115

AUTUMN

To Market, to Make It 131
Apples to Apples 147
The Great Pumpkin 161
In Touch with Your Roots 175

WINTER

Winter Wonderland 191
Cookie Exchange 209
Soup's On 221
Heartwarming 237

Resources 251
Index 253

About the Photographer 257
About the Author 258

Introduction

AS SOMEONE WHO HAS been planning, and dreaming about, and pining for, and otherwise been completely enthralled with the world of entertaining for as long as I can remember, having the occasion to write a book on the topic has felt like an absolute dream come true. Clearly, at some point, perhaps while rummaging around in an antique or thrift store, I must have rubbed an oil lamp and unleashed a genie that quietly, covertly, stealthily granted me the wish of a lifetime.

I have spent the past year hosting parties. In my garden, on my porch, in the field down the hill from our home, atop a mountain ridge, cozied up beside the fireplace—anywhere a party could be thrown, I've likely done it. Over the course of twelve months, I have had the immense pleasure of mixing and mingling, noshing and chatting, crafting and festooning with friends and family, again and again. We've witnessed the seasons shift, enjoyed delectable foods, laughed a great deal, and shared in experiences that will not soon be forgotten.

There was definitely a good bit of strategy involved. There was also elbow grease. There was even some heavy lifting. What there was most of all, though, was fun. So much fun. These parties, they began to be about much, much more than what was unfolding on a literal level. Each one, in its own distinct, unique way, began to take on an almost sacred quality, with its own degree of reverence and mindfulness. My guests and I were having a blast, and we were nourishing our bodies, but we were enriching our souls and our spirits too.

I come from a long line of entertainers. My familial ties don't lie in stage acting, or film, or playing musical instruments, though. The type of entertaining my kith and kin engaged in required the use of plates, utensils, and napkins. It typically involved donning fine clothing. Without question, it always, always involved laughter. You see, I hail from a lineage of culinary and social enthusiasts. A love and abiding passion for dining and cooking and rubbing elbows (and wiping mouths!) with a throng of others is in my DNA. Whether we're talking about a leisurely brunch, a noontime tea, or an impromptu evening of cocktails and nibbles, my people, they do so very much like to gather and dine.

I've long heard mention of the elaborate black tie and evening gown midnight feasts my bridge-playing paternal grandparents hosted. For years I've witnessed my father and his wife host block parties and Christmas gatherings and Easter brunches and casual dinners with equal aplomb. From my mother I've listened to recounts of fondue parties long since passed, and born firsthand witness to epic holiday meals. Birthdays were met with annual lily gilding, complete with glorious cakes. Sunday suppers were the stuff of legends. Family weddings would have set the feasts and debauchery of Dionysian legend to shame. This penchant for partying, it runs deep.

When I met and married my husband in 2007, I discovered a true partner. I quickly learned that he was just as enamored with entertaining as I was. Beginning with our wedding, we have hosted every gathering we could come up with. A Mad Scientist Halloween Party? Check. A Return to Childhood 25th Birthday Party for a dear friend (complete with mini hamburgers, cupcakes, a Slip 'N Slide, and a game of tug-of-war)? Done. We cooked up heaping platters of food and poured generous glasses of wine, punch, and beer for our nearest and dearest, year after year, season after season.

Along the way, however, we began to realize something. While hosting these gatherings brought us immeasurable joy, they were rather costly to pull off on our own. Why not ask our friends to provide some of the food or beverages, allowing the fun to continue while offsetting a bit of the expense? Which is precisely what we did. The idea for a monthly "Supper Club" series was hatched. Cooking, and hosting twenty friends for, a meal based on the cuisine of Cyprus, or India, or Argentina sounded like so much fun—and so much money. Instead, we asked friends to each

bring a country-specific dish and a bottle of wine or six-pack of beer to share. Everyone dined and imbibed with delight without emptying their wallets in the process.

This book is an extension of that spirit of collaborative dining we put in motion all those years ago. In the following pages, you'll find sixteen potluck parties built around the rhythm of the seasons. Food, décor, crafts, and more are part of each event, all collectively assembled and executed. You and your loved ones will be throwing memorable gatherings together, enabling everyone involved to have a wonderful time while sharing the responsibilities. Potlucks have saved the day for me, and for many other hosts hoping to pull off a diverse and abundant feast.

THE SPIRIT OF POTLUCK

We live in a time of incredible access to food. Across the globe, supermarket shelves offer eight brands of ketchup, canned pineapple in chunks, rings, dice, and crushed

forms, and entire aisles devoted to frozen desserts. You want strawberries in January? No problem. Coconuts in Canada? Consider it done. In today's modern food world, shoppers can find pretty much whatever they want, whenever they want it. Food is abundant and available and ready for purchasing at a moment's notice. There are even twenty-four-hour grocery stores, ready to accommodate a midnight craving for doughnuts or hot dogs.

Clearly, this hasn't always been the case. Before the advent of refrigeration and petroleum-fueled vehicles, foods were largely regionalized, seasonal, perishable, and, during harsh weather, scarce. Careful planting and planning for off-season eats was crucial to survival. If your larder and root cellar weren't packed to the gills with canned berries and chutneys and pickles and winter squashes and apples come December, you'd be staring down a long, cold, hungry winter.

All of this advance preparation was especially handy when dealing with unexpected guests, and played into the origins of the word *potluck*. Literally meaning "the luck of the pot," potluck dishes were offered to guests one hadn't anticipated hosting a meal to. What they were fed was determined by what one had available, tantamount to a sort of culinary crapshoot. If your guests showed up during the summer, when the garden was growing full throttle, the hens were laying, and the cow was offering milk, wonderful! If they happened to stop by one snowy winter evening, though, then their luck of a robust meal was to be determined by the thrift and knack for planning of their host.

Over time, the term came to be more closely associated with habits practiced in potlatches. A type of festival involving gifts and food practiced by native peoples of the Pacific Northwest, potlatch gatherings were held during winter months and were spiritual, culinary, and economic in nature. Host families invited guests into their homes and gifted them in song, dance, food, and other items, such as the sharing of natural resources. Intended as a means of wealth redistribution and asset equality, hosts gained status and upped their social ranking directly in relation to the inherent value of the gifts they gave.

This notion of sharing and gifting with what one had worked its way east over time. Potlatch practices merged with the potluck's "work with what you've got" ethos, resulting in the modern understanding of the term. Today's potlucks are often edible mash-ups, with a bit of this, a bit of that, and everything in between for the choosing. The cost of hosting a meal to a large number of guests gets distributed (much like in a potlatch) and has been fused with the "we'll eat whatever we're presented with" character of potlucks. The result is a thoroughly modern take on communal eating.

For better or for worse, however, modern potlucks have developed a bit of a pejorative connotation among those who consider themselves serious devotees of food. And perhaps for good reason. I can't begin to count the number of times I've worked with attention and precision and love over a dish only to arrive at a potluck and find store-bought chips and hummus and packaged cookies as other guests' contributions. It's disheartening and, often, not particularly tasty.

Potlatches and potlucks have a shared history in giving of oneself. Following in that vein, this book seeks to reclaim the spirit of nourishing ourselves and others. Food is central to our very survival. Taking of what we have and giving it freely rewards us long after the meal has passed.

BRINGING IT ALL HOME

In these pages, you'll find recipes, crafts, and décor that highlight the delicious bounty and stunning visuals of the four seasons. Since I base my meals at home around the growing season and the calendar year, structuring *Handmade Gatherings* in a similar manner made perfect sense. Frosty winter fetes, lush springtime soirees, sultry summer get-togethers, and crisp autumn affairs—it's all here. With sixteen themed gatherings, there's sure to be something to please every palate and satisfy every preference.

To get you started, I'm sharing my tried-and-true tips for pulling off great parties. From how to be a great host (page xvii) to the best ideas for collectively pulling off beautiful décor (page xxvi) and crafts (page xxviii), I'm offering up all of the party-throwing tools I've collected in my tool belt along my entertaining journey. And when it comes to the gatherings themselves, you'll find seasonal suggestions for working with the freshest, ripest foods and botanical elements to create gorgeous parties pulled off courtesy of a little help from your nearest and dearest.

Above all, my sincerest hope is that *Handmade Gatherings* conveys the belief I hold so dear when it comes to seasonal entertaining: when you gather together with others, with intention and vision and love, you'll be filling your bellies, yes, but you'll also be deeply nourishing your souls, and creating memories that'll far outlast the occasion itself. Sure, you're there for the food, but you're also gaining connection and community and camaraderie in the process. You're slowing down, as well, to cook, to notice the seasons, and to enjoy all of it in the company of others. And in that slowing down, in that deliberation, is where the magic happens, I've long felt.

When you move through life with a bit more calculated precision, you begin to notice the subtle flavor variations among apples at a gathering celebrating that fruit, or the way soup tastes better when you make a pot together, or the silliness and fun that erupt when dancing in an outdoor summer cakewalk. The seasons don't change overnight, and neither do we. When we slow down and notice the world unfolding around us, we experience awe. We might just gain a bit of clarity too. And we definitely find a comfort and solace that happen only when we take the time to allow ourselves to get caught up in the splendor of it all.

Gathering the Essentials

ANYONE CAN PUT A CALL OUT that a party is pending. What makes a gathering truly memorable, though, is the amount of thought put into its planning. The parties in this book were conceived as communal affairs. As such, you'll be sharing a great deal of the work with your guests, and there will be considerably less for you to do than if you were pulling it off alone. However, the devil, as it's said, is in the details. Careful, thoughtful advance planning will go far toward making the day an easy one for you and an enjoyable one for your guests.

Gatherings with loved ones should be a good time, period. That said, if a bit of party-throwing and party-attending etiquette is exercised, you'll all be more the merrier for it. Here we'll examine general tips for hosts and guests alike, as well as how to effectively communicate party-planning details, venue selection considerations, and food concerns, including allergies, safety, and transportation. Additionally, we'll look at how to decorate and craft collaboratively, including how to delegate purchasing or providing materials and dinnerware.

HOW TO BE A GREAT HOST

As I mentioned previously, in the final analysis, what you want guests to take away from your gatherings are wonderful memories of delicious food, pleasing environs and décor, and enjoyable company. There's a great deal everyone can do toward making that happen. The burden of pulling off such wonderful events isn't falling on just one person, as is often the case in entertaining. Working collaboratively, you and your guests can pool your resources, skill sets, and, yes, manners, to offer the parties of a lifetime. That said, the host is still responsible for many details: planning party specifics, inviting guests, and making sure everything is accounted for to make a successful party.

HOW TO COMMUNICATE WITH GUESTS

CRAFT THE RIGHT MIX OF GUESTS. Creating a memorable gathering involves a curatorial hand when it comes to the guest list. A room full of quiet folks presents just as great a challenge as a house packed with gregarious types. Consider personalities, ages, genders, and general interests (and disinterests) when deciding whom to invite.

SEND OUT A SAVE-THE-DATE. People's schedules fill up incredibly quickly these days. Sending a save-the-date e-mail three to four weeks ahead of the gathering is a good way of securing the date, especially for those events held close to popular holidays.

PROVIDE EVENT SPECIFICS ONE TO TWO WEEKS IN ADVANCE. Since these events involve specific culinary themes, as well as decorations and craft supplies your guests might need to procure, give them ample time to get everything together. Furthermore, as the gatherings are seasonal in nature, guests will need adequate time to get to area farmers' markets, farms, or their own gardens to collect the necessary ingredients. Detailed notes about the event's specifics should be sent no later than one week in advance, ideally two weeks.

KEEP COMMUNICATION OPEN—KNOW WHAT EVERYONE IS BRINGING. True, everyone is here for a good time. And while a good time can sometimes manifest as twelve pumpkin pies at a pumpkin-centered party, it's best to round out the dishes so that an entire meal is offered. Avoiding overlaps is a big concern when hosting a potluck. I speak from experience, when I once neglected to learn in advance what folks were bringing and ended up with a dinner party consisting solely of desserts. Specific dishes right down to their individual ingredients aren't necessary, but a general "I'm bringing a roasted beet dish" or "I'll be bringing some sort of chocolate cookie" works wonders toward preventing a one-course pileup. You'll hear me refer to this

many times throughout the book, for good reason. Keep in touch with your guests to know who's bringing what.

BE COMFORTABLE MAKING REQUESTS. If one guest has already indicated they'll be bringing deviled eggs to a southern foods potluck and another states the same intended dish, it's all right to guide them in a different direction. Unless the dish is highly personal ("But these are my great-grandmother's deviled eggs!"), most guests are more than happy to switch gears and bring something else.

GIVE DETAILED DIRECTIONS, TIMES, AND DATES. When sending out information in advance of the gathering, be sure to provide the event's specifics. Location, directions, time, and date should be given to guests in your detailed correspondence (but not in the save-the-date notification). That way, guests know what's in store, and you don't have to run interference replying to multiple solicitations for further information.

HAVE A BACKUP PLAN. There are some guests who are going to eat a lot of food—a whole lot of food. Despite the unspoken rule of only taking a bit so that others farther down the line might have some to enjoy, sometimes folks just find that pulled pork too tempting to take only one spoonful. As the host, it's your responsibility that no one goes hungry. While you certainly can't please everyone, keep some extra cheese and crackers or homemade pickles or dip on hand should the table suddenly appear rather scarce.

HAVE A WING MAN/WOMAN. Perhaps you love entertaining but are a bit of a shy guy. Or maybe you know yourself well enough to anticipate a near panic attack just prior to your guests' arrival. Get yourself a wing person! That is to say, enlist a spouse, significant other, sibling, friend, or neighbor who knows you well and can address the crowd if you're feeling sheepish or can locate the backup cooler on their own to ice down the beer.

HOW TO COMMUNICATE EFFECTIVELY

The most effective means I've discovered for communicating all of the details of hosting gatherings is digital. Online correspondence is immediate, and it allows guests to reply at their convenience. Furthermore, there's typically a great deal of back-and-forth, as folks determine what dish they'll be bringing and ask questions. Here are the three best online methods I've found for event correspondence.

1. E-mail: I use e-mail often for event planning. It's fast, convenient, and perhaps the easiest means of communicating, as it doesn't involve creating any external pages or images. That said, it is the most basic, in terms of appearance, so keep that in mind when selecting which means of correspondence you'd like to use.

2. Facebook event page: Creating a Facebook event page is a great way to keep everyone in clear, open, accessible communication. You can even create an event page with an image or graphic design if you'd like and post it along with the event details.

3. Evite or similar online invitation sites: I've been using Evite almost as long as it's been around. The site contains premade graphic invitations with a wide variety of motifs to choose from. You can also upload your own design if you prefer.

HOW TO CHOOSE AN IDEAL VENUE

CONSIDER THE NUMBER OF GUESTS. Select a location that can accommodate everyone invited. Being squeezed into a tiny apartment for a winter party with twenty guests doesn't read "cozy," it reads "cramped." Similarly, a gathering for four in a covered picnic pavilion for one hundred won't be intimate enough to evoke the right mood.

CONSIDER THE NEEDS OF GUESTS. If you have someone with bad knees or an arthritic hip, a mountaintop might not be the best location to host your picnic gathering. Those with small children, seniors, or pregnant women might not appreciate a summer event in a sultry location without shade. Keep in mind those on your guest list when choosing your site and always bear in mind their individualized concerns.

CONSIDER UNEXPECTED LOCATIONS. I've hosted potlucks on mountaintops, in fields, and in gardens. We've held them on porches, in apple orchards, on patios, and around campfires. All of which is to say, when selecting a location for your gathering, think beyond the dining room. Indoor gatherings around a table are lovely, but they're not the only place memorable get-togethers can take place.

KEEP CHILDREN IN MIND. While some gatherings will be perfectly suited to children, others won't. If you're hosting, keep this in mind and plan child care as needed. If you're attending, inquire as to whether children are welcome.

KEEP ANIMALS IN MIND. I live in a dog-loving area. It's completely normal for friends to show up with their dogs in tow. For some gatherings, their presence was completely appropriate for the occasion, while for others, I advised friends in advance to leave their four-legged friends at home. If you're a dog person, check with your host first before showing up with Fido. Also, if you have known pet allergies, ask the host if they have pets and medicate yourself as needed. Keep in mind that a courteous guest won't show up at a house with dogs and ask them to be put outdoors.

HOW TO ADDRESS FOOD ALLERGIES AND FOOD SAFETY

HAVE GUESTS DETAIL THEIR DISHES AT THE GATHERING. Sensitivity to guests' dietary concerns is a wonderful thing to bear in mind. That said, if there are vegans, vegetarians, carnivores, and lactose-intolerant and gluten-free guests all in the mix, it's inevitable that not every dish offered will work for everyone. To that end, assemble everyone around the table holding the food prior to eating. Ask guests to share what they've brought. Not only is it lovely to hear all of the stories behind why guests brought the dish they did, it's also helpful to other guests with specific diets or food allergies. At all of my gatherings, just prior to eating, we would all come to the feasting table and share, in the round, what we brought and why. It was wonderful to hear the stories of heirloom and much-loved recipes and to learn exactly what ingredients were in each dish.

LABEL DISHES WITH EGGS, DAIRY, NUTS, OR GLUTEN, IF DESIRED. After everyone is assembled and has detailed their dish, feel free to label items with small tags if they contain a known allergen. E (eggs), D (dairy), N (nuts), G-F (gluten-free), and V (vegetarian) written on a small label and set in front of dishes containing those foods will do the trick if you think it's necessary to do so. Otherwise, guests with known food sensitivities can glean that information when everyone is sharing their dishes and talking about the ingredients they contain.

KEEP COLD FOODS COLD. Food safety is just as essential as food flavor. You don't want to host a gathering wherein the most memorable aspect after the day has passed is that folks got sick. Cold foods should be kept chilled during transport and remain chilled until they are served.

KEEP HOT FOODS HOT. The same issue applies with foods that need to be served warm. Bacteria grow and thrive between 40°F and 140°F. If foods requiring cold or heat for food safety are left out at room temperature, they shouldn't remain so for more than two hours. This is crucial to ensure food safety.

ALWAYS HAVE WATER ON HAND. While many gatherings will have alcoholic beverages offered, it's inevitable that some guests won't be consuming them. Always be sure to have water available. It's all right if it's not ice cold at all times, but it should be in an obvious, convenient location for anyone needing it.

HOW TO BE A GREAT GUEST

While the host is the one organizing the event, guests certainly play considerable roles at these gatherings too. Consider them the supporting actors to the host's lead, the Robin to their Batman. To that end, here are some tips I've learned in my party-hosting

and party-attending history that'll go far toward ensuring you continue receiving coveted invitations to memorable gatherings for years to come.

RSVP. If I were the type to hold grudges (which, thankfully, I'm not), it would be the grudge of habitual non-repliers. Letting the host know whether or not you'll be coming is hugely assistive to them. If you're undecided, do them the courtesy of informing them that's where you currently reside on the attending/not-attending spectrum. I speak from repeat experience when I say it's enormously frustrating to have to steadfastly ask guests whether or not they're attending. A simple "yea" or "nay" (or "I don't know yet!") is all that's needed to engender goodwill with your host.

MAKE AN EFFORT. These gatherings are special occasions, and should be treated as such. There's a time and a place to bring chips and salsa to a gathering, but this isn't necessarily it (unless the chips are homemade and the salsa was made with ripe, fresh backyard tomatoes). A bit of effort on your part shows the host you appreciate all they've done to involve you in this event. It also shows the other guests you understand the significance of the occasion and are interested in honoring their attendance (and efforts) as well.

OFFER TO HELP. One of the best parts of hosting a potluck gathering is that the amount of work typically performed by a host is reduced considerably. As a guest, you don't necessarily need to staff the bar or man the grill, but simple things like washing up your dishes or at the very least bringing them to the sink go a long way toward helping the host want to throw another collaborative gathering. Ask the host if there's anything you can do. They may decline your offer, but they'll absolutely appreciate it.

BRING A SERVING UTENSIL. Much like showing up to a dinner party with a bouquet of flowers but no vase in which to house them, arriving without a serving utensil to a potluck throws your host a curveball. Now, a seasoned host will have a reserve of serving utensils for the utensil-less set in the mix. Many hosts, however, are new to the game of entertaining (I'm thinking specifically of college students or young folks on their own for the first time) and might lack things as basic as extra serving spoons or pie servers. Bring your own and remember to retrieve it when you depart.

GIVE THE HOST A HEADS-UP IF YOUR DISH HAS "SPECIAL NEEDS." It's fine if you need to chill your watermelon on-site or want to warm up your soup at the host's house. Just give them advance knowledge of your dish's needs, so they're prepared to turn over the stove or oven or provide space in the freezer or fridge. Most hosts will anticipate a need for something along these lines, but the courtesy of a heads-up will be greatly appreciated.

DECORATING AND CRAFTING COLLABORATIVELY

One of the most distinguishing factors of this book, I feel, is that right alongside sharing the supply of food at parties is sharing in the decorating and crafting. This helps the host to do things up while keeping costs down. When everyone is involved in each aspect of throwing an event, there's a greater sense of personal obligation and commitment. Furthermore, when all hands are on deck, the day gains greater significance and meaning to each person present, creating lasting memories. It's not just the host's responsibility to pull off a great get-together; it's up to each person attending to make it wonderful. Here are my tips for making that happen, when it comes to collaboratively creating the gathering's look and activities.

SHARING THE DÉCOR

As the host, you get to choose the look. That said, if you're truly interested in working with others, feel free to solicit feedback from guests in your save-the-date correspondence.

After you've selected the aesthetic you have in mind, be sure it involves a bit of decorating everyone can realistically do together. In other words, you don't want to ask guests to bring a décor element that is prohibitively expensive to purchase or difficult to obtain. For each gathering featured here, I've given décor suggestions that are all affordable and readily available, regardless of location. As you use this book as a source of inspiration for crafting future seasonal, collaborative gatherings, keep those elements in mind.

Remember, guests will need adequate time to source and procure the decorative

elements you ask them to supply. That's why the correspondence containing all of the event's details should be sent out at least one to two weeks prior, with two weeks being the preferable amount of time. With that in mind, as the host, try to have some extra decorative elements on hand. Some guests are bound to forget their décor at home, so having extra will allow them to still participate while keeping the look full and well fleshed out.

SHARING THE CRAFTING

Each of the sixteen gatherings offered here features a seasonally thematic craft. For some of the crafts, I've supplied the materials, while for others, guests brought supplies. It will be up to you, the host, to know what you're able to provide, based on your personal craft supplies and what you'll need help with.

Don't be shy if you end up needing your guests to help you provide everything to pull off the craft. Some folks will have a wealth of supplies on hand, while others (again, I'm thinking of college students and young folks here) will have precious little. It's all right to ask for help—that's what these gatherings are all about, pooling resources to create wonderful, meaningful, memorable events.

Remember, again, to give ample time for guests to pick up their crafting materials. The same applies to you as well. If you're making the root beer syrup for the In Touch with Your Roots gathering, everyone will need plenty of time to source the herbs the beverage requires, as well as get their hands on a small glass bottle for taking home their portion. That's why advance planning is so very key to pulling off these parties without a hitch.

SHARING THE DINNERWARE

As a veteran entertainer, I've got multiple platters, several sets of dinnerware, and a medley of table linens. I assume myself to be the exception, and not the rule, however, when it comes to having an arsenal of tableware on hand. Bear in mind your personal provisions when planning these gatherings and plan accordingly.

To that end, if you're hosting ten but only have enough silverware for six, ask guests to bring some with them. A mishmash of cutlery, or napkins, or dinner plates, or wine glasses for that matter, only serves as a testament to the spirit of togetherness pervading these gatherings.

If you have a specific look in mind for a gathering, it's all right to ask guests to bring their dish in a container fitting that aesthetic (e.g., white bowls for a winter gathering, or green dishes for a spring soiree). Keep in mind, though, that some guests may not have such a dish on hand. You may need to be able to provide those serving dishes yourself in this case, so factor that into your plans and make adjustments as necessary.

SHARING THE TABLESCAPE

Tablescape is a term describing the manner in which elements on a table are displayed; tablescapes done collaboratively can be beautiful things to behold. The sum often being greater than its parts, table arrangements done in concert with others are often quite stunning. Many of the gatherings in this book involve guests bringing natural, found objects with them to the parties and then carefully placing them together on the table in an arrangement. Allowing the process to happen organically, without micromanaging or implementing a heavy hand as the host, presents an opportunity for a gorgeous display to develop.

The way the dishes themselves are arranged on the table is another element of the tablescaping process. Be mindful of both form and function when placing platters or bowls of food on the table. Drippy sauces shouldn't be placed too far back on the table, while a towering platter of rolls at the front might block access to other dishes. Allow guests to place their dishes where they like, but feel free, as the host, to move things around as needed. The placement of a dish by the first guest to arrive might have made sense at that time, but less so right before the meal is served.

Consider a variety of heights for creating visual interest on the table. Cake stands or overturned terra-cotta pots are great for this purpose. Creating vertical space not only makes things more visually arresting, it also opens up lower level areas for fitting more on the table. You can supply these vertical elements, or ask guests to bring them along with their dish if they have them.

SPRING

Spring to Life

Ushering in a much-needed dose of green, spring is a wondrous time of year. This party is a great way to welcome the change of seasons and remember that hope springs eternal.

IT'S EASY TO FORGET, during the dark days that come with colder weather, that the Earth is still very much alive. The barren tree branches, withered plant stems, and frozen-over puddles, ponds, and lakes characterize the landscape. It seems as though vigor, growth, and vitality have all fled the scene, leaving only stillness, quiet, and dormancy in their wake. This gathering, then, is a wonderful reminder that still waters truly do run deep. Though it appears that all is at rest, the reality is that the natural world is quite active—within trees, beneath the soil, and, yes, even in those frozen ponds. By celebrating the return of new light and new life, you and your guests will have the opportunity to gain a renewed appreciation for the fortitude and perseverance of nature. It may also be the perfect way to shake off those last dark days of winter and inspire hope by acknowledging the light to come.

Several years ago, I happened to be in New York City in May. It was just a short trip there and back, literally a mere twenty-five hours from the time my plane landed in Newark until I was on the return flight home. After checking in to my hotel, I headed out to meet some friends for lunch. I recall it being an absolutely flawless spring day. Manhattan couldn't have been lovelier. The sky was blue, there were a profusion of strollers out cruising the city streets, and even the characteristic quick, frantic pace typically associated with the Big Apple seemed a bit slower, a tad more subdued.

The restaurant I was meeting my friends at was situated across the street from a smallish city park. It was teeming with life that day. What caught my attention the most, though, were the flowers. The park was riddled through with tulips. Red, yellow, pink, purple, orange—every hue of tulip imaginable was represented. When I saw those flowers swaying gently in the urban spring breeze, I remember having this realization that hope really does spring eternal.

Those flowers are members and residents and citizens of the city too, it suddenly occurred to me. They're growing and moving and changing just like everyone else. They have seasons of growth and seasons of dormancy; times when they flourish and thrive, and times when they rest and slumber. The spring tulips of New York City helped me realize that we're all connected—humans, animals, trees, soil, everything. Some of us run around this Earth untethered, while others, like my revelatory tulips, hold tight to this planet, reemerging each spring to once again have their moment in the sun.

Even when things seem still and quiet and immobile, there's often much going on just beneath the surface. This gathering, then, is my homage to those tulips viewed that fateful day. They helped me remember that recovery and renewal and restoration are possible, even in places that at times are so removed from the natural world. When I threw this gathering, it was a warm, beautiful May day. My friends and I couldn't stop talking about how good it felt to be back outside and the thrill we all felt at the blooms and buds and greenery and growth surrounding us. May you and your guests feel the change the new season is ushering in and relish in its possibilities.

SETTING THE SCENE

This party is an ideal opportunity to celebrate the birth, growth, and renewal that characterize the season. You and your guests can make the vitality and hopefulness of spring come to life with a few simple decorative flourishes.

LUSH AND VIBRANT COLORS: Create an enlivening atmosphere by bringing in the colors of the season—verdant greens, bright yellows, and the gentle browns of the earth waking up.

BRANCHES AND BLOOMS: As there is an absolute profusion of near-to-bursting blooms and buds on branches this time of year—from apples to quinces, cherries to forsythias—ask guests to bring a branch of whatever they come across. Either they can bring a water-filled vase for forcing blooms or you can provide a variety of vessels for placing the branches in upon their arrival.

A BREATH OF FRESH AIR: This gathering would be lovely hosted in a space that invites the fresh, enveloping breezes and scents of spring. A porch, patio, lanai, picnic pavilion, or similar space that offers protection from spring rains, should they occur, while also allowing ample airflow is a perfect location to consider.

SHARING THE EXPERIENCE
MAYPOLE DANCE

The traditional Maypole dance would be great fun at this gathering. Emblematic of renewal, fertility, and protection, the dance is enjoyed by traditions the world over. A pole, such as a broomstick or thick wooden dowel, is erected, and ribbons are strung out from its top. As participants dance, they weave around one another, representing the merging of humans and the natural world.

MAKE SEED STARTS

Let's truly celebrate the return to verdant life by planting seeds and watching them grow and thrive! Newspaper seed starts are inexpensive to create and easy to construct. Make as many starts as you and your guests need to send everyone home (and leave the host) with a few of each seed being planted.

YOU WILL NEED

- Black-and-white newspaper
- Bag of potting soil
- Spring seeds (consider peas, fennel, dill, lettuce, and leafy greens)

TO MAKE

Begin with a sheet of black-and-white newspaper (I used a 22 x 11.5-inch sheet). Fold the sheet in half at its crease. Fold the creased sheet in half again, at its width. Fold the paper in half one last time.

Using a drinking glass or other cylinder as a guide (I used a half-pint mason jar), form the newspaper into a circle. Remove the jar from the paper.

Tuck the ends of the newspaper into one another, creating a secure hold. If you need to provide further support, you can tie a piece of garden or butcher's twine around the pot's circumference (you may need to momentarily slip your drinking glass or jar back into the pot's opening to provide support as you tie the twine).

Now to make the pot's base. Take a sheet of newspaper and squeeze it as tightly as possible, forming a ball. Place it in the bottom of the pot. Using your drinking glass or jar, press down on the balled paper as tightly as you can, flattening it out.

Fill your pot with potting soil and seeds. If you're starting only one pot, place it on a saucer. If you're making a number of pots, place them on a tray. Water very gently.

Once your seeds have sprouted and the weather reaches the right conditions for planting, you can transition your pots outdoors. Simply dig a hole deep enough to accommodate the planter, lining up the top of the soil in the pot with ground-level soil. The newspaper will rot away over time and the root system on bottom needn't be disturbed.

COOKING IT UP

Spring is when many a home cook sighs a collective breath of relief. The root vegetables that sustain so many of us all winter long begin giving way to a host of leafy, light spring greens and vegetables. Radishes, new potatoes, peas, carrots, spinach, lettuce, beets, broccoli, dill, leeks, scallions, asparagus, and watercress are welcome sights in backyard gardens and at farmers' markets. As the stems of rhubarb ripen and strawberries sweeten over their beds of straw (that's where their name originally came from!), fruits begin making their way back into the home cooking repertoire as well.

MENU SUGGESTIONS

Pistachio-Crusted Asparagus with Feta Vinaigrette*,

Honey-Roasted Carrots and Peas with Tarragon*, Strawberry Galette with Mint Whipped Cream*,

Rhubarb Buttermilk Bread*, Rhubarb Crisp, Chicken Potpie, Strawberry Bread Pudding,

Lamb Kebabs with Mint Pesto, Roasted Herbed Potato Salad, Spinach Soufflé, Buttered Radishes,

Beet and Blue Cheese Salad, Spring Crudité Platter, Spring Onion Tart, Fried Chicken

PISTACHIO-CRUSTED ASPARAGUS WITH FETA VINAIGRETTE

Don't be surprised if you're tempted to eat this entire dish yourself. I speak from experience: My husband and I fully intended to eat this over the course of several days;
it was so good, however, that we polished it off in one sitting. The interplay of tart

and sweet flavors in the vinaigrette and the crunchy and smooth textures in the nuts and asparagus satisfied just about every type of food craving it's possible to have, all in one delicious dish.

Serves 4 to 6

++++++++++++++++++++++++++++++++

YOU WILL NEED

2 pounds large asparagus

¼ cup olive oil

1 cup shelled pistachios

1 teaspoon sea salt

2 tablespoons crumbled
   feta cheese

1 tablespoon chopped
   fresh parsley

FOR THE
VINAIGRETTE

¼ cup olive oil

¼ cup crumbled feta cheese

2 teaspoons lemon
   juice

2 teaspoons red wine
   vinegar

1 tablespoon honey

Several grinds of black
   pepper

++++++++++++++++++++++++++++++++

TO MAKE

Preheat the oven to 400°F.

Rinse the asparagus and cut about an inch off of the stem ends. Pat the asparagus dry.

Place the asparagus on a dry baking sheet, put in the oven, and bake for 3 minutes to dry off any excess moisture. Remove the sheet from the oven and toss the asparagus on the sheet with the olive oil.

Crush the pistachios in a food processor (or under a towel with a kitchen mallet or hammer) for about 1 minute, until finely ground. Transfer the ground nuts to a small bowl. Using a spoon or clean hands, mix the nuts with the salt.

Lay the asparagus out evenly across the baking sheet. Sprinkle the spears with half of the ground pistachio and salt mixture. Turn the spears over, then evenly sprinkle them with the rest of the ground pistachio mixture. Bake for 10 minutes, then remove from the oven and, using tongs, carefully plate the spears onto a platter.

Combine all of the vinaigrette ingredients in a lidded container or a food processor. Shake or process until smooth. Drizzle the plated asparagus with the vinaigrette. Top with the feta and parsley. Serve at room temperature.

HONEY-ROASTED CARROTS AND PEAS WITH TARRAGON

++++++++++++++++++++++++++

YOU WILL NEED

2 tablespoons olive oil

2 tablespoons unsalted butter

¼ cup fresh tarragon leaves

1½ pounds carrots, cut into ½-inch discs

¼ cup honey

1 pound green peas, cooked

1 teaspoon sea salt

Several grinds of black pepper

++++++++++++++++++++++++++

We had a friend visiting when we were working on this recipe. She'd brought her four-year-old daughter, who offered to serve as a taste tester. Her repeated requests for "more, please" and declarations of "I've never had anything so good!" should definitely serve as testament to the flavor wallop this dish presents. Even better, it's really pretty too!

Serves 4 to 6

TO MAKE

Heat the olive oil and butter in a medium saucepan over medium heat. When the butter is fully melted, place the tarragon leaves in the pan, spreading them out. Cook for about 30 seconds. Remove the leaves from the pan and drain them on a paper towel.

Add the carrots to the pan and cook for 10 minutes, stirring occasionally. Stir in the honey and cook for 7 to 8 minutes until slightly caramelized. Turn off the heat; add the peas, salt, and pepper and stir to fully combine. Add the tarragon leaves and stir a bit more. Spoon into a bowl and serve.

STRAWBERRY GALETTE WITH MINT WHIPPED CREAM

While there's little that can be done to improve upon the sublime perfection that is a ripe strawberry, a bit of time in the oven and some mint whipped cream certainly don't hurt. This galette (simply a dishless pie) comes together so quickly you'll be finding occasions to make it all season long.

Serves 6 to 8

YOU WILL NEED

FOR THE WHIPPED TOPPING

- 1 cup heavy cream
- 2 tablespoons finely chopped fresh mint
- 3 tablespoons powdered sugar

- ½ recipe Basic Pie Dough (recipe follows)

FOR THE STRAWBERRY FILLING

- 1½ pounds strawberries
- ⅓ cup plus 1 tablespoon granulated sugar
- 2 tablespoons arrowroot or cornstarch
- Zest of 1 lemon
- 2 teaspoons vanilla extract

FOR THE EGG WASH

- 1 egg yolk
- 1 tablespoon cold water

╬╬╬╬╬╬╬╬╬╬╬╬╬╬╬╬╬╬╬╬╬╬╬╬╬╬╬

PREPARE THE WHIPPED TOPPING: Combine the heavy cream and mint in a lidded container, such as a mason jar. Shake the contents vigorously. Place the mixture in the refrigerator and steep for at least 4 hours or up to 8 hours.

PREPARE THE CRUST: Remove 1 disk of the chilled pie dough from the refrigerator. Roll out the dough into a 12-inch circle on a lightly floured surface.

Transfer the pastry dough to a large baking pan lined with baking parchment. Place the pan in the refrigerator to chill while preparing the filling.

PREPARE THE FILLING: Rinse, hull, dry, and cut the strawberries into ¼-inch-thick slices. Combine ⅓ cup of the sugar, the arrowroot, lemon zest, and vanilla in a large bowl. Add the sliced strawberries. Using either clean hands or a mixing spoon, toss the ingredients together until the berries are completely covered by the dry ingredients.

ASSEMBLE THE GALETTE: Preheat the oven to 375°F.

Carefully fan out the strawberry mixture in concentric circles with the tips pointing toward the center of the pastry circle. Begin about 2 inches from the pastry edge, overlapping the fruits as you move toward the center. Fold up the border, overlapping the pie dough and pressing folds together every few inches.

PREPARE THE EGG WASH: Beat together the egg yolk and water. Brush the folded crust edges with the egg wash. Sprinkle the remaining 1 tablespoon sugar evenly across the pie dough edge. Bake for 30 to 35 minutes, until the crust is golden and the filling is bubbly in the center. Cool the galette for at least 30 minutes before serving.

Strain the contents of the jar containing the cream and mint through a fine-mesh sieve. Discard or compost the mint. Using either a mixer or whisk, beat the infused cream with the powdered sugar until billowy peaks form. Serve alongside the pie.

BASIC PIE DOUGH

Makes crust for 1 double-crust pie

TO MAKE

Mix the flour and salt together in a medium-large bowl. Using a pastry cutter or 2 forks, incorporate the butter until the mixture resembles a coarse meal (you should still have rather large bits of butter when you're done). Slowly drizzle in the ice water. Stir with a mixing spoon until the dough starts to clump.

YOU WILL NEED

2½ cups all-purpose
   flour
1¼ teaspoons sea salt
 1 cup (2 sticks) unsalted
   butter, chilled and
   cubed
¾ cup ice water

Transfer the dough onto a floured work surface and fold it together into itself using your hands. The dough should come together easily but should not feel overly sticky. Cut the dough in half and shape it into 2 balls. Wrap each dough ball in cellophane and refrigerate for at least 1 hour.

Proceed according to the galette recipe instructions above, using one dough disk and freezing the other.

RHUBARB BUTTERMILK BREAD

I didn't grow up in a household that ate rhubarb. Which is a shame, considering all the years lost on opportunities for enjoying this tart, versatile "fruit." As one of the only fruit options available come early spring, it's a welcome sight to behold in backyard gardens and area farmers' markets alike. Here I've partnered the puckery fruit with lemon zest, vanilla beans, and hazelnuts. Welcome to your new favorite springtime quick bread!

Makes one 9 × 5-inch loaf

Preheat the oven to 350°F. Generously butter a 9 × 5-inch loaf pan and set it aside.

PREPARE THE TOPPING: Place all of the topping ingredients in a medium bowl. Using clean hands, mix everything together until the ingredients are fully combined and the butter is in pea-size clumps. Set aside while you prepare the bread batter.

PREPARE THE BATTER: Combine the flour, sugar, baking powder, baking soda, and salt in a medium bowl, using either a whisk or a fork. Add the eggs, buttermilk, melted butter, lemon zest, and vanilla bean seeds. Whisk together until the ingredients are fully combined.

With a mixing spoon, stir in the chopped rhubarb until it is well blended into the batter.

ASSEMBLE THE BREAD: Pour the batter into the prepared pan. Use a spatula to evenly distribute the batter across the surface of the pan. Sprinkle the topping evenly across the batter.

Place the pan into the oven. Bake for 1 hour, or until the top is golden and a knife inserted into the center of the loaf comes out clean. Cool on a wire rack for at least 30 minutes before serving.

Note: To remove the seeds from a vanilla bean pod, using a pointy-end knife, slice the pod open lengthwise, then scrape out the tiny seed flecks with the knife tip.

YOU WILL NEED

FOR THE TOPPING

- ¼ cup all-purpose flour
- 2 tablespoons brown sugar
- 3 tablespoons unsalted butter, cubed
- ¼ cup chopped hazelnuts
- ½ teaspoon ground nutmeg

FOR THE BATTER

- 1½ cups all-purpose flour
- ¾ cup granulated sugar
- 1½ teaspoons baking powder
- ¾ teaspoon baking soda
- ½ teaspoon sea salt
- 2 large eggs
- ½ cup buttermilk
- 6 tablespoons unsalted butter, melted
- Zest of 1 lemon
- Seeds from 1 vanilla bean (see Note)
- ¾ cup chopped rhubarb

Wild Things

The untamed life that evidences in spring is a glorious thing to behold. This gathering celebrates that independent, intrepid spirit that pervades the season.

THE COLD IS WANING, the days are lengthening, and the wild things are again on the move. From fungi to frogs, daffodils to dandelions, creatures underfoot and overhead from field to forest, stream to sea are poking up through the soil, scurrying about, and ripening on branches. An exploratory walk among these busy, growing beauties packs a massive sensory punch. Textures, tastes, sights, sounds, and scents permeate the landscape, making us feel truly alive. A gathering celebrating a full embodiment and awareness of wild spaces sets the stage for profound experiences, like an acknowledgment of the order that pervades in even the wildest settings or the few footsteps away from such an untamed existence we maintain.

It also invites and encourages stewardship of these fragile, fleeting habitats. A number of the guests at the gathering I hosted, including myself, shared how pleasantly surprised we all were to find that foraging itself heightened our awareness of our natural surroundings, leading to unexpected discoveries. Deep in concentration, on the hunt for wild foods, my friends described noticing, for the very first time, just how much acorn tops look like tiny fairy hats, or discovering the intense camouflage of a toad resting beside the rotted log they were foraging morels near.

There is something so majestic, so magical, so freeing and uncensored, when in the presence of wild things. I live in a secluded, forested mountain cove. We're tucked a mile down a dirt road on eleven acres, with hundreds of undeveloped swaths of land flanking our little homestead. Accordingly, run-ins with and sighting of wild creatures are a regular occurrence here. From black bears to coyotes, massive snapping turtles to raccoons, opossums to wild turkeys, deer to hawks, if it's wild and native to the area, chances are I've had a brush with it out here. Those chance encounters always leave me a bit breathless. My pulse raises, my heart rate accelerates, my vision gets sharper, my hearing a little clearer. I'm not scared, really. Exhilarated is closer to the truth.

So, too, with walks in the forest, or along the coast, or atop a mountain, or in a se-

cluded valley. These chance glimpses of wild creatures leave me humbled. A great deal of modern living is planned and orchestrated and, often, predictable. In spaces that haven't undergone human alteration, every action and occurrence is unscripted and unplanned, at least from my vantage point. Rocks tumble and are jostled and jolted into action in creek beds during violent rainstorms. Birds appear from out of thin air, nibbling at greenery or excavating a worm. Butterflies move suddenly from flower to bush to hedge.

To the flowers and the fungi, the rivers and rocks, the frogs and fawns, it's all as it should be. For us, though, it's a glimpse into a parallel universe, unfolding and occurring in tandem with our own, and yet worlds away from it. There's order, of course, and there's some inherent predictability too. The sun rises, the sun sets. The creatures forage at night or during the day. The fern fronds unfurl in early spring and cast off their spores in autumn. When you observe natural spaces, you plug into a rhythm you otherwise miss, a tune you might not hear if you're not carefully paying attention.

When I was about twenty-two years old, I read Annie Dillard's essay "Living like Weasels." Describing a chance encounter with a weasel at a suburban pond she frequents, the author relayed a sense of wanting to live as the weasel lives, out of necessity, and not of choice like humans. She writes, "*We can live any way we want. People take vows of poverty, chastity, and obedience—even of silence—by choice. The thing is to stalk your calling in a certain skilled and supple way, to locate the most tender and live spot and plug into that pulse. This is yielding, not fighting. A weasel doesn't 'attack' anything; a weasel lives as he's meant to, yielding at every moment to the perfect freedom of single necessity.*" Those words forever altered the course of my life, as I realized all we stand to learn from paying close attention to the "wild ones" in our midst.

SETTING THE SCENE

Wild-crafted treats of the forest, field, sea, and mountains are what's in order for festooning this gathering. This is an ideal occasion to let your decorating imagination run wild!

A WILD PALETTE: Let the natural world serve as your color consultant for this party. From the soft taupe of a wild mushroom to the gentle brown of a turtle shell, take your cues for linens and tableware from earthy hues of the world around you.

THE GREAT OUTDOORS: Encourage guests in advance of the day to pick up a few this and thats for adorning the feasting table while out foraging edibles for their dish. Rocks, flowers, branches, bits of moss, feathers, seashells, leaves, butterfly wings, cicadas, edible mushrooms, twigs, seaweed, abandoned snail shells, seed pods, turtle shells, nut shells, clover, and any other wild item ethically collected would be welcome additions to the gathering table.

WIDE OPEN SPACES: A gathering that celebrates the wild world we live in should naturally take place out in it. A forest clearing, creekside grassy patch, seaside or lakeside area, and even simply the wildest part of your or a friend's or loved one's yard would all be ideal locations to consider.

TWILIGHT MAGIC: This party would be absolutely breathtaking if it took place around sunset, when the wild world seems its most magical. Lanterns, hurricane lamps, oil lamps, luminaries, and torches would be whimsical lighting elements to consider.

SHARING THE EXPERIENCE
THE THRILL OF THE HUNT

After the guests have assembled and eaten their fill, gather together and encourage folks to share their foraging experiences. It can be so enlightening and captivating to hear others' stories of what they brought, where they foraged, unexpected discoveries as they hunted, and creatures they witnessed along the way.

CRAFT CORSAGES AND BOUTONNIERES

Create wearable décor and wardrobe embellishments for the event in the form of corsages and boutonnieres. Encourage guests to bring a few extra bits of foraged vegetation with them. During the gathering, set up a station with their harvests, along with floral

YOU WILL NEED

- A minimum of 3 floral and/or botanical elements (see Note)
- Binding material, such as bouillon wire, light-gauge wire (26 to 29), jute, twine, raffia, or floral tape
- Pearl-headed corsage pins (for pinned corsages and boutonnieres)
- Ribbon (for wrist corsages)

tape, wire, jute, raffia, twine, ribbon, and pins. You may even want to whip up a sample, so that guests have a sense of how it's done. Guests can then bring their corsages and boutonnieres home for pressing. Later, long after the gathering has passed, the pressed memento will serve as a beautiful testament to the splendor of the day, and the bounty that can be found on our verdant planet.

TO MAKE

Begin by placing the focal flower in your hand, and then tuck the other floral elements around it. Keep in mind that boutonnieres and corsages look best if some elements are higher in the arrangement, while others are situated a bit lower (i.e., try to avoid placing them all in a straight row). Leave at least 3 to 4 inches of stems intact before cutting the arrangement.

Holding the arrangement in one hand, use your other hand to wrap about 2 to 3 inches of the stems in either bouillon wire, light-gauge wire, jute, twine, raffia, or floral tape (the choice is entirely up to you and is simply a matter of personal aesthetic preferences; they all do the same job in the end, which is what's most essential). Leave several inches of stem exposed so that you can place the boutonnieres and corsages in water once wrapped without getting the wrapping material wet.

If making wrist corsages, the same instructions apply, only with bigger, fluffier, "frillier" elements. For wrist corsages, wrap the stems in ribbon after first securing them with wire or floral tape and then tie onto the wrist.

When you're ready to pin the boutonnieres or corsages, trim the stem ends. Use a pearl-headed corsage pin and affix the arrangement to the wearer's left shoulder. Guide the pin through the back of the garment, across the arrangement on a diagonal, and out again through the front side of the garment.

Note: Your chosen 3 (or more) elements should consist of varied textures and colors if at all possible. One element will be the focal flower, so it should be larger or more visually arresting than the others.

HOW TO ETHICALLY AND CONSCIENTIOUSLY WILD-CRAFT EDIBLES

- Be mindful of where you forage. Many protected natural areas have prohibitions on wild-crafting. If you're on private land (that you don't own) or public lands, check beforehand to see if foraging is permitted.
- Gather only a few plants, fruit, fungi, or nuts, so that others may forage and also to keep the plant from being overforaged.
- If there is only one plant or specimen in an area, leave it.
- Use clean scissors or a knife when harvesting so that diseases aren't spread from one one location to another. Cut or shear instead of tearing or pulling to minimize plant damage.
- Harvest fungi by twisting it gently from the stem and lightly pulling.
- Steer clear of contaminated areas, like roadsides.
- Pay attention to the vegetation underfoot when foraging, taking care not to trample it or disturb delicate ecosystems as you gather.
- Do not dig anything up; take only the outermost leaves, fruits, and nuts so that the plant can reproduce the following year.
- Eat only those plants, berries, fungi, or nuts you are certain are safe to eat. Making a guess can result in sickness or, in rare circumstances, death.
- A number of wild foods are endangered or rare, needing conservation, not harvest. Read up in advance on what's in abundance and what's scarce in your area and pick accordingly.

Gathering foods from the wild is a transformative experience. What may have previously appeared as simply a beautiful landscape suddenly materializes into a living pantry. Using my suggestions for ethically, and safely, wild-crafting edibles, you'll discover a cornucopia of delectable eats. Once you start foraging, you'll never again view wild settings through the same lens. There's a whole world out there, just waiting to be tasted!

MENU SUGGESTIONS

Morel, Caramelized Onion, and Mozzarella Frittata*, Wildflower Risotto*,
Quick Pickled Ramps*, Fiddlehead Fern Salad, Warm Potato and Ramp Salad,
Chickweed Pesto Pasta Salad, Sautéed Dandelion Greens and Herbs,
Dandelion Head Fritters, Stinging Nettle Ravioli, Lamb's Quarter Pizza,
Dandelion Wine, Wild Mushroom Pâté, Yarrow Tea

MOREL, CARAMELIZED ONION, AND MOZZARELLA FRITTATA

This frittata makes the most of those precious, fleeting wild mushrooms of spring—morels. Partnered alongside buttery, creamy caramelized mushrooms and crowned with fresh mozzarella, each bite will no doubt put an extra "spring" in your step!

Serves 2 to 4

TO MAKE

Cook the bacon in an oven-safe 12-inch skillet over medium heat until lightly crispy. Remove the bacon and set aside. Add the diced onions to the pan and cook for about 5 minutes.

YOU WILL NEED

2 slices of bacon (see Note)

½ large onion, diced

1 cup beef stock

½ teaspoon sugar

1 tablespoon unsalted

butter

A handful of chopped

wild-foraged morels

6 large eggs

¼ cup milk

Pinch of sea salt

Several grinds of black

pepper

2 to 3 ounces

fresh mozzarella

cheese

Add the stock and sugar. Cook for 25 to 30 minutes, until the onions are caramelized and there is no more liquid in the pan. Remove the onions from the pan and set aside.

Preheat the broiler. Add the butter to the skillet and, when melted, add the morels. Cook for about 5 minutes, then remove the morels from the pan and set aside. Turn the heat down to low. Whisk the eggs in a bowl with the milk, salt, and pepper. Add the egg mixture to the pan and cook for 3 to 4 minutes, until the eggs just begin to set. Meanwhile, cut or tear the bacon into bite-size pieces. Distribute the bacon, morels, onion, and mozzarella across the top of the eggs. Remove the pan from the stovetop and place under the broiler for 2 to 3 minutes, until the eggs are set and the cheese begins to melt. Remove from the oven and let it sit for a few minutes. Invert the frittata from the pan onto a platter, then invert it onto another platter so that it is right side up again. Cut with a pizza wheel and serve.

Note: If you'd like to make this dish vegetarian, simply omit the bacon, add 2 tablespoons of olive oil to the pan, and replace the beef stock with vegetable stock.

WILDFLOWER RISOTTO

A risotto crowned with wildflowers packs a massive sensory punch. I used violets and apple blossoms here, but whatever is fresh, available, and edible in your area will work just as well. If at all possible, pick the wildflowers just before serving the risotto, so that they'll still be colorful and vibrant when placed atop the dish.

Serves 4 to 6

TO MAKE

Cook the bacon in a medium pan over medium heat until it starts to get crispy. (For this recipe, I used a cast-iron skillet, as I love that it can go directly from the stovetop to the table.) Remove the bacon from the pan and set aside. Drain about half of the bacon fat, then add the diced onions. Cook the onions, stirring occasionally, for 10 minutes. Add the rice and cook for another 5 minutes, stirring frequently.

Add 1 cup of stock and stir into the rice. Stir nearly constantly, without stopping for more than 20 seconds at a time. Whenever the liquid level gets low, add another ½ cup of the stock. Add the wine in place of the stock one of those times, if using.

After the rice is cooked fully but still has a bit of bite (after about 40 minutes of cooking), add the Parmesan, herbes de Provence, crumbled bacon, pepper, and salt. Cook for about 5 more minutes, leaving it a little looser than you would serve it, because it will tighten up as it cools.

Sprinkle the flowers over the top of the dish. Serve at the table in the pan.

Note: If you'd like to make this dish vegetarian, simply omit the bacon and replace the fat with 3 tablespoons cooking oil, and use the vegetable stock.

YOU WILL NEED

3 slices of bacon (see Note)

½ medium onion, diced

2 cups Arborio rice

6 cups hot chicken, ham, or vegetable stock

½ cup wine (or additional stock)

½ cup grated Parmesan cheese

1 tablespoon herbes de Provence

A few grinds of black pepper

Pinch of sea salt

Edible wildflowers to cover the risotto (about 1 cup)

QUICK PICKLED RAMPS

These refrigerator-pickled ephemeral treats are the essence of springtime. Paired with fresh cilantro, garlic (another allium!), lemon zest, and spices, they're perfect for dunking into a Bloody Mary or martini. They're also delicious served on an antipasto platter alongside hard salumi slices, cornichons, and pickled beets (another springtime crop).

Makes one 1-pint jar

TO MAKE

Bring the vinegar and water to a boil in a medium saucepan. Stir in the salt and sugar until dissolved. Remove the brining solution from heat.

Meanwhile, blanch the ramps for 2 minutes in boiling water, then drain. Fill a pint-size jar with the ramps. Add the peppercorns, cumin seeds, celery seeds, mustard seeds, hot pepper flakes, cilantro, and lemon zest.

Pour the brine over the ramps. Screw a lid onto the jar and refrigerate for at least 3 days or up to a few weeks before eating.

YOU WILL NEED

¾ cup white vinegar

¾ cup water

2 teaspoons sea salt

2 tablespoons sugar

20 to 30 ramps (enough
    to fill a pint jar),
    cut into 3-inch
    lengths

2 teaspoons peppercorns

1 teaspoon cumin seeds

1 teaspoon celery seeds

1 teaspoon mustard seeds

½ teaspoon hot pepper
    flakes

2 tablespoons chopped
    fresh cilantro

A few small strips of
    lemon zest

The Good Egg

Eggs have long served as a harbinger of spring. This party celebrates the birth, growth, and renewal that spring epitomizes.

EGGS HAVE BEEN ENJOYED, revered, and honored by humans for millennia. Powerhouses of nutrients encased in a protective shell, eggs have been fried, scrambled, poached, pickled, boiled, and so much more ever since that fateful day a primitive ancestor discovered a nest of them and became curious. And how very grateful we modern folk are for that ancient inquisitiveness. Eggs are now an integral part of the culinary repertoire and décor of countless cultures the world over. A gathering based around eggs is sure to satisfy the palate, enliven the visual landscape, and imbue the event with a great deal of fun.

All manner of fowl gain their cues to lay eggs by the amount of sunlight they receive. Before the creation of electricity and its by-product, artificial timed lighting in henhouses, egg-laying birds would taper off their egg production as the days grew shorter and the nights more chilly. Much like squirrels and other creatures that are stimulated in their pituitary glands to store up food or taper off certain activities by waxing and waning sunlight, most fowl naturally curtail egg output during the winter months. As such, come springtime, when the days once again lengthen, eggs would make their debut in nests of all persuasions.

Those were happy days for our ancestors. That revelry evidenced itself in celebrations, activities, and foods honoring all things egg. From egg hunts and tosses to chocolate eggs and Fabergé eggs, the egg is globally entrenched in myriad cultures. The Christian holiday Easter has even incorporated egg-based elements into its canon. The modern English *Easter* derived from *Eastre* or *Eostre*, meaning an Anglo-Saxon goddess representative of "light" and "dawn" and "to shine." All of which makes perfect sense when consideration is given to the essential role that sunlight played in civilizations prior.

Eggs are also, quite clearly, emblematic of fertility and life and abundance. The fact that, within its fragile shell, the conditions for creating life are present is a thing of wonder and awe when you take the time to stop and consider it. All of this latent potential exists, much akin to the oak lurking inside of the acorn, or the future fruit-bearing tree inside a tiny apple seed. Eggs feed, they give life, and they sustain it, all within a thin wall of protection.

Taking the time to stop and acknowledge this fact proved incredibly powerful when I was planning the gathering. As I chatted with guests at the party, several mentioned having been moved by the mindfulness with which they approached the topic too. Thinking so concertedly about potential and possibility was incredibly inspiring, we all found. Maybe we're not in the career we'd imagined we'd be in at this time in our lives, or perhaps we're frustrated with some other as yet unachieved goal. The egg shows us that hope isn't lost, that there's a world of potential resting quietly within.

In modern times, with our abundance of conveniences, it's easy to forget just how much all the life around us moves in a perpetual dance and rhythm with the natural world. A gathering that draws attention to eggs and all that they offer and represent is a wonderful opportunity for experiencing gratitude for what we have today, and what our ancestors experienced in their own time. We may have moved far from the days of roughing it in the great outdoors, but we're still tethered to this planet and all of the creatures we cohabitate with on it. Eggs can keep us grounded, humble, and eternally thankful.

Give your loved ones something to cluck about at this gathering. Fun, festive, and lighthearted, this party acknowledges the seasonal shift with whimsy and delight.

SHELL SHOUT OUT: From the faintest cream shell to the richest brown, consider incorporating eggshell colors into your décor. Robin's egg blues and soft olives appear in eggshells too, and would be lovely worked into this palette.

ALL THINGS EGG: Since this gathering is an homage to all things egg, ask guests to bring whatever egg references might be feathering their own nests. Nests, feathers, egg-collecting baskets, paperweights, marble eggs, candied eggs—any item that gives a nod to the world of eggs is welcome. The items can be distributed decoratively around and about the food tables.

FOWL LANGUAGE: I've kept a flock of laying hens and one rooster for several years. I also live in a forest loaded with wild birds. Between the two, if there's anything I've learned from the avian life out here it's that they're a chatty bunch. Lively, animated, and always, always making some sort of cluck or trill or squawk or maw or similar sound, no doubt about it, fowl are talkative. As the host, do whatever you can to encourage conversation at your gathering. If you have a shy buddy, seat them next to the most gregarious guest on hand. Or toss out questions to the crowd that encourage fun banter, like celebrity gossip or popular TV show trivia.

SHARING THE EXPERIENCE

EGG ROLL

An egg roll is a great means of injecting your gathering with some silliness. In this game, participants must roll a hard-boiled egg across a grassy area, using either a spoon or, for the more intrepid, their noses. Whoever finishes first wins! Guests young and old can get in on the action with this game, although I'd advise not mixing ages in the same race, so as to give everyone a fighting chance at winning!

MAKE SILK-DYED EGGS

Silk-printed eggs have been used in seasonal decorating for centuries. All that's needed is some 100 percent silk fabric, some eggs, rubber bands, and vinegar. Scour thrift stores, or your own clothing collection, for scarves, ties, boxers, blouses, or other items made of silk. If you'd like to keep the dyed eggs for use next year, blow out the insides of the eggs first.

YOU WILL NEED

- Large white eggs
- Scissors
- 100 percent silk fabric
- Plain muslin or old white
  cotton sheet or pillowcase
- Rubber bands or twist ties
- Large stockpot
- ¼ cup vinegar
- Vegetable oil (optional)

Cut swatches of silk big enough to cover the egg smoothly and tightly, about 6 to 8 square inches per egg. Cut muslin or cotton swatches to the same size.

Wrap the eggs completely in the silk, making sure that the printed part of the fabric faces the egg, and secure the silk with a rubber band. Wrap each silk-wrapped egg in a piece of muslin, sheet, or pillowcase, and secure it with a rubber band as well.

Place the wrapped eggs in a large stockpot and cover with water at least 2 inches above the eggs. Add the vinegar. Bring the water to a boil, then reduce the heat and simmer for 20 minutes.

Remove the eggs from the pot and let cool on paper towels or an old dishcloth. Unwrap the eggs, and if you'd like a little shine, rub each egg with a drop of vegetable oil.

Since eggs are commonly used in cooking, a feast based around their use presents countless means of incorporating them into a dish. Literally running the gamut from (egg drop) soup to (sugar-coated) nuts, the entire culinary and dining spectrum can be represented here. As with other gatherings, it might be good to have guests detail what they're thinking of bringing in advance, so as to ensure the full range of dining options is represented.

MENU SUGGESTIONS

Bacon and Caramelized Onion Egg Salad*, Lemon and Dill Deviled Eggs*,
Strawberry and Lemon Curd Pavlova*, Ham, Egg, and Cheese Casserole,
Asparagus and Feta Quiche, Caramelized Onion Frittata, Challah,
Orange and Almond Flan, Egg Custard Pie, Strawberry Macaroons,
Herbed Egg Noodle Salad, Scotch Eggs, Sugared Pecans

BACON AND CARAMELIZED ONION EGG SALAD

Since bacon and eggs are a natural pairing, and onions are an indication that spring is officially here, marrying the three together seemed like a good idea. Oh, and how! A bit of thyme gives an herbal edge to this creamy, crispy, salty bowl of deliciousness.

Makes 3 cups

TO MAKE

Heat the olive oil in a medium sauté pan over medium heat; add the onions and sauté for about 10 minutes, until they start to brown a little around the edges. Add the stock and cook for about 30 minutes, until the liquid has almost all evaporated.

YOU WILL NEED

2 tablespoons olive oil	⅓ cup mayonnaise
1 large onion, diced	¼ cup sweet pickle relish
2 cups chicken, beef, or vegetable stock	1 tablespoon prepared mustard, such as Dijon
12 hard-boiled eggs, peeled	2 teaspoons dried thyme
3 slices of cooked bacon, crumbled	Several grinds of black pepper

Continue cooking for another 10 minutes, stirring frequently so the onions don't stick, until they become caramel colored. Let the onions cool while you prepare the eggs and cook the bacon.

Chop the eggs into small pieces and place them in a mixing bowl. Add the onions and the rest of the ingredients and mix well. Serve immediately or place in a lidded container in the refrigerator and eat within 2 to 3 days.

LEMON AND DILL DEVILED EGGS

Deviled eggs are always a hit at parties. They're delicious and easy to hold, and they can be consumed in one bite. Here I've included dill and lemon, flavors long associated with spring.

Makes 2 dozen deviled eggs

YOU WILL NEED

12 hard-boiled eggs

 2 tablespoons mayonnaise

 2 tablespoons extra-virgin olive oil

 2 tablespoons Dijon mustard

 2 tablespoons sweet pickle relish

 1 teaspoon lemon zest

 1 tablespoon minced fresh dill

Sea salt and cracked

   black pepper to taste

Dash of hot sauce

Small sprigs of dill (optional), for garnish

Remove the shells from eggs; rinse each egg under cold water. Cut the eggs in half lengthwise. Carefully remove the yolks and transfer them to a medium bowl; set the whites aside. Add the remaining ingredients to the yolks; mix with a fork or whisk until creamy and light.

Fill a pastry bag with the mixture and pipe the filling into the egg-white halves, or simply portion the filling out with a spoon into each halve. Top each egg-white half with a few dill leaves, if using. Refrigerate the eggs until ready to serve. They taste best if first allowed to come to room temperature. They will keep refrigerated for up to 2 days.

STRAWBERRY AND LEMON CURD PAVLOVA

What could be more delicious than a dessert with a meringue crust and a marshmallow center? Add lemon curd, a creamy whipped topping, and fresh spring strawberries and you've just about reached dessert perfection!

Serves 6 to 8

TO MAKE

PREPARE THE LEMON CURD: Wash and dry the lemons, then zest them, taking care to avoid removing any pith along with the zest. Set the zest aside. Juice the lemons and strain the juice over a fine-mesh sieve to remove any membranes or seeds. Set the juice aside.

Break the eggs into a medium metal bowl and beat lightly to incorporate the whites into the yolks. Fill a medium saucepan with about 2 inches of water and place over medium heat. Bring to a gentle simmer.

Put the bowl filled with the eggs on top of the pan of gently simmering water to form a double boiler. Add the sugar, butter, lemon juice, and lemon zest and whisk gently until the sugar dissolves and the butter melts. Stir the mixture with a wooden spoon until it thickens and coats the back of the spoon, 8 to 10 minutes. Remove the curd from the heat. Transfer to a lidded container. Leave at room temperature while you prepare the rest of the recipe.

PREPARE THE MERINGUE: Preheat the oven to 250°F. Place the oven rack in the center of the oven.

Line a baking sheet with baking parchment. Use either a mixing bowl or a compass to draw an 8-inch circle in the middle of the parchment. Flip the parchment over so that the drawn side faces down on the baking sheet but is still visible through the paper.

In a large bowl, beat the egg whites on medium speed until foamy peaks appear. Increase the speed to high and gradually beat in the sugar until the mixture becomes stiff and glossy, 6 to 8 minutes. In a small bowl, whisk together the vinegar, vanilla, cornstarch, and ¼ cup of the beaten egg and sugar. Add the mixture to the rest of the beaten egg in the mixing bowl; beat on high speed for 3 to 4 minutes, until firm, stiff peaks appear.

Pile the meringue onto the parchment circle. Dab small bits of meringue onto the underside of the four corners of the parchment to keep it secure. Use a spoon to spread the mixture into an 8-inch circle and make a small indentation in the

YOU WILL NEED

FOR THE LEMON CURD

6 large lemons

4 large eggs

2 cups superfine sugar (see Note)

10 tablespoons unsalted butter, chilled

FOR THE MERINGUE

4 large egg whites

1¼ cup superfine sugar (see Note)

1 teaspoon white or apple cider vinegar

1 teaspoon vanilla extract

1 tablespoon cornstarch, arrow root, or potato starch

FOR THE WHIPPED TOPPING

2 cups heavy cream

1 tablespoon powdered sugar

1 teaspoon vanilla extract

FOR THE TOPPING

2 cups fresh strawberries, sliced

meringue circle (this is where the lemon curd, whipped cream, and fruit will go once the meringue is baked).

Place the baking sheet in the oven; bake for 1 hour, or until the meringue appears dry and very pale in color. Turn off the heat, leave the oven door slightly open, and allow to cool completely.

PREPARE THE WHIPPED TOPPING: Combine the heavy cream, powdered sugar, and vanilla in a mixing bowl. Beat on high speed until billowy clouds of cream appear. Set aside.

ASSEMBLE THE PAVLOVA: Transfer the meringue from the parchment to a serving platter. Mound the lemon curd in the center of the meringue. Use a spatula to spread it around evenly. Pile the whipped cream on top of the lemon curd. Use the spatula to distribute it evenly. Top the whipped cream with the sliced strawberries. Serve immediately, or refrigerate and serve within several hours.

Note: If you can't source superfine (caster) sugar, simply pulse granulated sugar in a food processor several times until it becomes more fine and then measure from there.

Pollinating Ideas

The buzzing, flying activity of pollinators makes the season truly feel alive. This party serves as a nod to and endless "thank you!" for all of that industry and labor.

AS A BEEKEEPER, I've had the exquisite pleasure of witnessing firsthand just how very busy those winged beauties are when trees and flowers are in bloom. It's truly humbling when you stop and consider the astounding fact that forager honeybees visit between 150 and 1,500 flowering plants daily in their quest for nectar and pollen. Such work, such industry! Their connection to their bodies and to one another is absolutely essential in ensuring both individual and collective survival. They're a unit, those bees, working in glorious, harmonious, fastidious concert. This gathering acknowledges the crucial service they provide to the many foods we love and celebrates the cooperative spirit they exemplify.

We are enormously fortunate that honeybees and their pollinating colleagues are so enamored with and devoted to their task. Hummingbirds, butterflies, moths, wasps, beetles, bats, flies, and a host of other creatures of the sea, soil, and air work diligently and steadfastly at pollination. As they go about the business of gathering food sources for themselves and their coinhabitants, they simultaneously perform a massive task benefiting all life on Earth. Most creatures on this planet rely on plants for food, shelter, and oxygen. In order for these creatures to survive, it's then absolutely essential that plants are able to reproduce and continue to offer them sources of nutrients, housing, and more.

Plant reproduction occurs via pollination, a process wherein pollen grains, which are the male germ cells of plants, are moved to the stigma, the tip of the plant's female reproductive part. About 90 percent of flowering plants need animals to aid in their pollination. That's where these ever-essential pollinators step in, moving from flower to flower in search of nectar, a rich food source secreted from glands in the plant and nestled in the flower's blossom. As pollinators hunt and search for the nectar, they rub against the pollen grains. When the pollinator then moves on to an-

other part of the plant, or visits a new plant, these grains are moved onto the stigma, eventually forming a seed.

All of those busy, busy bodies in motion are gathering not just food but information too. They then disseminate it to their colleagues back in the hive. Whenever a forager discovers a food source, as soon as it returns to the hive it shares the news by way of some strategic dance moves. Moving in a circle or a figure eight, the bee is able to relay, with a pretty good deal of precision, the location of the cache. The configuration of the dance is informed by the distance required to reach the food source. If the nectar supply is a vast and abundant one, the dance is a bit more intense, the moves a tad more vigorous.

The big win for us humans is that pollinators do all of this work for the overall good of all life for free. Scientists estimate that one out of every three bites of food we consume is made possible through pollination, as is between two-thirds and three-fourths of all cultivated foods humans consume. That's a colossal amount of food. From the foods we rely on to the foods and habitats that other beings on our planet depend upon, pollinators are the best friends to have, make, and keep. The Xerces Society, a nonprofit organization, works tirelessly toward this goal on a global scale. I invite you to check them out at xerces.org for tips on promoting pollination.

Pollinators, in addition to keeping us all fed and thriving, also offer up an incredible model for living. Through precise, conscientious, concerted dissemination of something they themselves require, they benefit everyone else in the process. That came up a lot at this gathering, this notion of "paying it forward" and selfless yet self-serving motivation. In between bites and sips of foods made available to us by the tireless efforts of pollinators, we savored the lesson to be gleaned from helping ourselves and others with each action and decision.

I love this idea of benefiting others as we better ourselves. I've long held the belief that, as we work toward bettering ourselves, our families, our communities, and our planet as a whole benefit. If I plant a flower or vegetable garden for my personal use, I'm enriching the neighboring ecosystem in the process. Or if I encourage my son to

be an empathic person, sensitive to the needs and feelings of others, there's a benefi-
cial long-term ripple effect there too. As it's said, what goes around comes around. In
following the model of pollinators, our comings and goings could make for a better
world, which sounds really, really good to me.

SETTING THE SCENE

This party is all about catching a buzz—a passion-for-pollinators buzz, that is. From
the festive colors pollinators are drawn to, to the delicious range of foods they're responsible for pollinating, there's plenty to celebrate!

A RIOT OF COLOR: Many insects, including wild pollinators, are able to view ul-
traviolet light, which humans aren't able to detect without special equipment. This
wide range of colors, many of them quite vivid, can be incorporated into the color
palette of the party. That means a range of reds (which attract butterflies and hummingbirds) or blues, violets, purples, and yellow, which beckon our bee friends. This
palette can be incorporated into everything from the linens to the plates and platters.

WILDFLOWER BOUQUETS: Ask each guest to bring a small bouquet of wildflowers
in a vase. If you'd prefer, you can ask guests to all use a similar-style vase (e.g., a glass
jar or a white vase). Otherwise, guests can choose any type of vessel they prefer. Bouquet size is also entirely at the discretion of each guest. Trust me when I assure you
that the final result, clustered together on the food table, will be gorgeous. The variety of vessels, flowers, and loving souls who fashioned them will make every guest
beam with happiness and, quite possibly, entice a pollinator or two to drop by for a
visit!

GARDEN OF DELIGHTS: It only makes sense to host a party all about pollinators
in an area they're drawn to. Consider hosting this gathering in a park, botanical
garden, flower garden, large kitchen garden, or any other area with abundant botanicals.

SHARE A "POLLINATING" IDEA

We can learn a lot from the pollinators in their "bettering others while bettering themselves" mission. To that end, ask guests to come with one "pollinating" idea to share. It can be any little thing that they're currently doing, or hope to do, or have heard about, that spreads and disseminates something that is for the betterment of our verdant planet.

MAKE POLLINATOR SEED PACKETS

A wonderful way to benefit pollinators while enjoying the gathering is to assemble seed packets. Tossed into their backyards or abandoned green spaces, or potted for balcony or apartment growing, the plants that grow, and the pollinators they attract, will serve as a living testament to the gathering's mission.

YOU WILL NEED

- A variety of seed packets (see Note)
- Small bowls for placing the seeds in
- Labels or placards for displaying seed names
- Mini craft envelopes
- Rubber stamp (optional)

Note: I used 2 to 3 packets of each variety so that there would be plenty of seeds available from each plant variety for each guest. For this gathering, I selected 6 plants: aster, buckwheat, green basil, lupine, purple coneflower (echinacea), and red clover. Make your selections from the following list of plants (seed packets for most of these are easy to come by at gardening and home supply stores, as well as online):

alfalfa, aster, bachelor buttons, basil (green), bergamot/bee balm, black-eyed susan, blanket flower, buckwheat, coreopsis, goldenrod, lobelia, lupine, mexican hat, milkweed, purple coneflower, yellow mustard

Open the seed packets. Place one variety of each seed in the small bowls. Make labels detailing what each bowl contains. Have guests pinch (or gather with small serving spoons or teaspoons) a few seeds from each dish and place them inside the craft envelopes. If you like, you can stamp the envelopes decoratively. I found the rubber stamp for this gathering from a seller on Etsy.

Seal the envelopes. Encourage guests to broadcast the seed packets somewhere they can visit, to enjoy both the beauty of the flowers and the pollinators happily enjoying their offering!

POLLINATOR CONSERVATION

Long after the party has ended, you can still work toward promoting stewardship of pollinators. Here are four helpful suggestions for fostering pollinator conservation from the Xerces Society:

1. Plant flowers, shrubs, and trees native to your area with overlapping bloom times. By having nectar available spring through fall, pollinators will be supported through the entire blooming season.
2. Provide places for pollinators to lay eggs. This can be achieved by building or purchasing bee nesting blocks or by leaving bare patches of ground, brush piles, or other wild spaces accessible where you live.
3. Avoid pesticide use. Insecticides and herbicides can reduce or eliminate nectar-producing flowers from the landscape.
4. Pollinate pollinator stewardship! Share the importance of pollinator conservation with your friends, family, and community.

In addition to, clearly, honey-based dishes, the following crops rely enormously on the efforts of pollinators: almonds, asparagus, blueberries, buckwheat, cardamom, carrots, celery, chocolate, coffee, fennel, strawberries, and vanilla, to name a few. All herbs available in the spring would be great to incorporate into a dish too. Indirectly, beef and milk are involved, as cattle consume alfalfa, another crop highly dependent on pollination. I've limited the list largely to spring crops, with some exotics added for flavoring considerations. Encourage guests to frame their dishes around these crops, if available. It's so much fun to see what everyone is inspired and motivated to cook!

MENU SUGGESTIONS

Spring Lamb Patties*, Buckwheat Salad*, Honey and Lavender Lemonade*,

Roasted Asparagus with Feta Vinaigrette, Honey-Glazed Carrots and Thyme,

Broccoli Slaw with Honey-Mustard Vinaigrette, Meatloaf with Honey Glaze,

Fresh-Baked Rolls with Almonds and Spring Herb Compound Butter,

Chicken with Almond Molé Sauce, Shaved Fennel Salad,

Pulled Pork with Blueberry Barbecue Sauce, Strawberry Shortcake, Mixed Berry Cobbler

SPRING LAMB PATTIES

These patties are rife with abundant, fresh spring herbs. They're also small, making them the perfect size for gatherings where multiple dishes will be served.

TO MAKE

PREPARE THE PATTIES: Finely mince the garlic and chop ½ teaspoon salt into it. Let the garlic and salt mixture sit for at least 10 minutes or up to 20 minutes. Meanwhile, cook the bacon in a skillet until crispy. Remove the bacon from the pan. Set the pan with the bacon drippings aside. Crumble the bacon once it's cool enough to handle.

Combine the crumbled bacon with the rest of the ingredients and the remaining 1½ teaspoons salt in a medium bowl. Form the mixture into patties about the diameter of golf balls. Cook the patties in the bacon fat over medium heat for 4 to 5 minutes on each side until slightly browned. Drain the patties on paper towels. Transfer to a large platter when ready to serve.

PREPARE THE TOPPING: Combine all of the topping ingredients in a food processor and process until just a little bit chunky; alternatively, use a mortar and pestle. Spoon a small mound of the topping onto each of the patties and serve.

FOR THE PATTIES

- 3 cloves garlic, peeled
- 2 teaspoons sea salt
- 2 slices of bacon
- 3 pounds ground lamb
- 1 cup chopped fresh herbs (choose from mint, rosemary, marjoram, thyme, lemon balm, sage, basil, parsley, and cilantro, in any combination)
- Juice from 1½ lemons
- 1 tablespoon fennel seeds
- Several grinds of black pepper

FOR THE TOPPING

- ⅓ cup capers
- 1 roasted red pepper
- 8 green olives, pitted
- Juice of ½ lemon
- ¼ cup olive oil
- Several grinds of black pepper
- 1 cup chopped fresh cilantro or parsley

BUCKWHEAT SALAD

It's easy to overlook grains when we think of the crops that pollinators assist. We'd be remiss in so doing, though, as their efforts save farmers billions of dollars. This dish combines buckwheat, which pollinators love, with several classic spring crops, including dandelion greens, peas, and mint. The dish is gluten-free, something that is always great to have at a mixed-dish gathering.

TO MAKE

Bring 4 cups of water to a boil in a medium saucepan. Add the buckwheat and stir. Cover, reduce the heat, and simmer for 20 minutes. Meanwhile, combine the chopped dandelion greens, 2 cups water, and wine in a medium sauté pan. Cook over medium heat about 20 minutes, until the liquid has evaporated. Remove from the heat and set aside.

Transfer the cooked buckwheat to a large bowl. Use a fork to fluff it up a bit. Stir in the cooked dandelion greens and the remaining ingredients and serve.

YOU WILL NEED

- 6 cups water, divided
- 2 cups buckwheat (one 16-ounce package)
- 1 bunch dandelion greens, chopped
- ⅓ cup wine
- 1¼ cups cooked peas
- 1 cup chopped fresh mint
- 4 ounces Serrano ham, chopped (optional)
- 6 ounces goat cheese, crumbled
- ½ cup olive oil
- ¼ cup white wine vinegar
- 1 teaspoon sea salt
- Several grinds of black pepper

HONEY AND LAVENDER LEMONADE

On a warm day, a glass of cold lemonade is about the most refreshing beverage imaginable. Add the ambrosial fragrance and flavor of lavender and honey and you've got just the thing to quench your thirst.

Combine the honey and water in a medium saucepan. Heat over medium heat until almost boiling, stirring to dissolve the honey into the water. Remove the saucepan from the heat. Stir in the lavender buds, cover, and let stand for 1 hour. Strain the honey lavender syrup and discard the buds.

Pour the syrup into a large pitcher or beverage dispenser. Add the lemon juice and stir. For every gallon your pitcher or dispenser will hold, add 5 cups of cold water. Stir to fully combine. When ready to serve, add ice cubes, lemon slices, and, if desired, a few fresh or dried sprigs of lavender.

YOU WILL NEED

1½ cups honey

6 cups water

2 tablespoons dried lavender buds (or 3 tablespoons fresh)

1¾ cups lemon juice

Ice cubes

Lemon slices for each glass

Lavender sprigs for each glass (optional)

SUMMER

Like a Rolling Stone (Fruit)

Lush, colorful, and watery, the stone fruits of summer are ideal foods for managing the heat of the season. This party celebrates the abundant sensory pleasures they provide.

WHEN IT COMES TO SUMMER, stone fruits are the unofficial mascot. From peaches and nectarines to cherries, plums, and apricots, the pitted, juicy bellwethers of the hottest season do much to assuage the tandem spike in mercury. While nearly the definition of gustatory perfection all on their own, stone fruits become achingly good when cooked. My idea for this potluck is to just cut to the chase and make it into a sweet pie party. You're already hooked, aren't you? A gathering paying homage to these fruits will, without question, be unfailingly delicious, delightfully messy, and so very much fun.

Members of the genus *Prunus*, stone fruits have long been revered and prized the world over. Mythology holds that peaches, native to China, were consumed by the immortals owing to their purported ability to impart longevity to anyone who ate them. Cherries were similarly given high status by both the ancient Chinese, who felt the fruits conferred immortality, and the Japanese, who associated them with beauty, modesty, and courtesy. So too with plums and apricots, fruits associated with virtues of love, beauty, and fertility.

Personally, stone fruits have captivated me for as long as I can remember. When I was younger, that owed in large part to their heady, ambrosial fragrance and exquisitely sweet flavor. As I grew older, though, what intrigued me more about these beautiful, delicious, sensory-walloping fruits was based on a less tangible aspect. It's in their pits that stone fruits have entranced me as an adult. The inherent ability to reproduce themselves, once coaxed out of their hard external shells, is completely exhilarating to me.

The fact that latent life exists inside these otherwise unremarkable-looking rigid pits is such a profound metaphor, if you consider it. Just to make it through our day-to-day reality, many of us have developed rough exteriors of our own. Much like these lovely fruits, though, we too can bring to fruition some incredible possibilities if provided the right encouragement. While the fruits need moisture and soil, we need determination, drive, and the courage to turn our convictions into realities.

When I was in middle school, I belonged to the Beta Club, an organization composed of students who exhibited high academic rankings. I was inducted into the club one fateful afternoon in the late 1980s. I'll never forget the ceremony, my mother proudly watching from the audience, the entire student body gathered in the school's auditorium while my fellow Betas and I stood on stage. My role in the ceremony was to light a candle, which represented "Initiative." With trembling hands, I lit the taper, saying aloud, "I light the candle for initiative," along with some words about why this trait was important.

That event would prove to be a formative one for me. Initiative, or taking the lead and activating change, is something I've been working on for decades. I was shy when I was younger, and keeping initiative and all of the potential the word radiated in my mind was essential for me. It drove me to make friends, explore hobbies and subjects that interested me, and step forward to learn, leap, and live.

At this gathering, held at a tiny mountaintop peach orchard with my friends, all of us feasting on stone fruit pies and relaxing on blankets, it dawned on me that that seed for initiative, planted in my adolescence, had actually come to fruition. My former self, so shy I could hardly stomach the idea of ordering a pizza over the phone, was holding court at a party, with comfort and ease. Much like the life and future generations of fruit lying dormant within peaches, nectarines, cherries, plums, and apricots, if we find the right setting and take the initiative, who knows what sort of harvest we might expect.

SETTING THE SCENE

A summer stone fruit potluck invites a casual, comfy vibe. Blankets, throw pillows, and a relaxed setting are what's needed to nosh in comfort.

THROW PILLOWS AND FRUITY BLANKETS: Ask guests to bring throw pillows and blankets in shades of plum, peach, apricot, and cherry, if they have them.

CELEBRATE SUMMER OUTSIDE: Make this an outdoor affair, and scatter the blankets and pillows around a soft, grassy area. If it rains, there's no need to change the plans—just move the party to an open space indoors and pile up the blankets and pillows on the floor!

PIE SERVERS APLENTY: Since there'll be a bevy of pies on offer, the proper tools for serving them will be in demand. As it's unlikely that you, the host, will have more

than one or two servers of your own on hand, ask guests to bring along a server or other serving utensil with them.

POT STONE FRUITS

Since several stone fruits have a long, storied association with longevity, a fun idea for a potluck in their honor is to send guests home with potted pits. Then they can begin their own orchard of stone fruits (or just stick with the one for the time being!). Inevitably, you will have gathered a collection of stone fruit pits when working on your recipes for the gathering. Remove them of as much fruit as possible, dry them on a baking sheet either in the sun or on the lowest setting on your oven, and reserve them for the potluck. Once guests arrive, have them pot the seeds in small, biodegradable cups (I used drinking cups purchased on Etsy), topped off with potting soil. Keep the pots moist and encourage guests to transfer them to larger containers when they return home.

MAKE PLUM LIQUEUR

What better way to preserve all of the sweet, nectary bliss of stone fruits at your gathering than to render them into liqueur? This recipe calls for plums, but you could easily substitute apricots, cherries, peaches, nectarines, or pluots. For an added flavor dimension, consider including a few whole cloves, cinnamon sticks, star anise, black peppercorns, allspice berries, or cardamom pods in the infusion.

Makes five 1-pint jars

YOU WILL NEED

2½ pounds plums, quartered
     (see Note)
2½ cups sugar
2½ cups vodka

TO MAKE

Fill each of five 1-pint jars about two-thirds full with the quartered plums. Add ½ cup sugar and ½ cup vodka to

each jar. Shake to combine. Store the plum liqueur in a dark, room-temperature location for 90 days. Shake the jar daily for the first week, then once weekly for the remainder.

After 90 days, strain the liqueur through a double layer of coffee filters. Discard or compost the fruit pieces. Use a funnel to transfer the liqueur to a sterilized glass bottle. Consume within 1 year.

Note: Reserve the pits from the plums and include them in the jar with the other ingredients.

COOKING IT UP

The stone fruits of summer are a gorgeous, juicy, ambrosial bunch. Peaches, apricots, plums, nectarines, and cherries are packed with quenching juices and sweet, delicious relief from the ravages of hot summer days in every bite. Their inherent high sugar content means they don't need too much additional sweetener when baked into pies. They do give off a good deal of liquid when heated, though, so be sure to include the proper amount of thickener called for in any recipe you're using. Ask guests to each bring a stone fruit pie. It's helpful to know in advance what everyone intends to bring so that you don't end up with ten cherry pies.

MENU SUGGESTIONS

Orange and Cinnamon Frangipane Plum Galette*, Crystallized Ginger Stone Fruit Potpie*,
Chocolate Cherry Hand Pies*, Cherry Pie with Coconut and Almond Topping,
Peach Cardamom Lattice-Top Pie, Plum Crisp Pie, Nectarine and Lavender Galette,
Apricot Mini Pies, Peach Chiffon Pie, Classic Sour Cherry Pie,
Plum and Allspice Cream Pie, Frozen Nectarine Pie, Apricot and Vanilla Crostata

ORANGE AND CINNAMON FRANGIPANE PLUM GALETTE

Frangipane is an almond filling, similar in flavor to marzipan but much softer and spreadable. Kissed with a hint of orange extract and ground cinnamon and crowned with fresh plum slices, this galette is equally delicious for breakfast, tea time, or dessert.

Serves 6 to 8

YOU WILL NEED

½ recipe Basic Pie Dough (page 17)

FOR THE CINNAMON SUGAR

¼ cup granulated sugar

1 tablespoon ground cinnamon

FOR THE FRANGIPANE
FILLING

1½ cups almonds

½ cup brown sugar

2 tablespoons all-purpose flour

1 teaspoon ground cinnamon

½ teaspoon sea salt

6 tablespoons unsalted butter,
 cubed

2 large eggs

2 teaspoons orange extract

1½ pounds plums, pitted and sliced
 into 6 pieces each

FOR THE EGG WASH

1 egg yolk

1 tablespoon whole milk

Preheat the oven to 350°F.

PREPARE THE PIECRUST: Remove 1 disk of the chilled pie dough from the refrigerator. Roll out the dough into a 12-inch circle on a lightly floured surface. Transfer the pastry dough to a large baking pan lined with baking parchment. Place the pan in the refrigerator to chill while preparing the filling.

PREPARE THE CINNAMON SUGAR: Place the sugar and cinnamon in a small bowl. Stir the ingredients together until fully incorporated. Set aside.

PREPARE THE FRANGIPANE FILLING: In a food processor, combine the almonds, brown sugar, flour, cinnamon, and salt and process until the almonds have broken down into very small pieces. Add the butter, eggs, and orange extract. Process until the mixture is smooth.

ASSEMBLE THE GALETTE: Mound the frangipane mixture in the middle of the chilled pie dough. Using a spatula, evenly spread the mixture toward the edge of the pastry, leaving a 2-inch border all around.

Gently press the plum slices into the frangipane, beginning with an outer circle and moving in to the center.

Fold up the border, overlapping the pie

dough and pressing the folds together every few inches. Beat together the egg yolk and milk. Brush the folded crust edges with the egg wash. Sprinkle the cinnamon sugar evenly on top of the crust edge. Bake for 40 to 45 minutes, until the crust is golden and the filling looks fluffy and is firm to the touch. Cool on a wire rack for at least 30 minutes before serving.

CRYSTALLIZED GINGER STONE FRUIT POTPIE

I love the concept of a sweet potpie. Who says all the goodness underneath a buttery, flaky crust needs to be savory? Here I've mixed peaches, plums, and nectarines with a hearty dose of crystallized ginger. The result is a perfect mix of sweet and spicy. While delicious on its own, this pie really shines with a dollop of whipped cream.

Serves 6 to 8

YOU WILL NEED

½ recipe Basic Pie Dough (page 17)

FOR THE FILLING

2 pounds peaches, peeled, pitted, and cut into ½-inch slices

1 pound plums, pitted and cut into ½-inch slices

1 pound nectarines, pitted and cut into ½-inch slices

⅓ cup arrowroot or cornstarch

½ cup sugar

¼ cup crystallized ginger, minced

½ teaspoon sea salt

FOR THE EGG WASH

1 egg yolk

1 tablespoon cold water

FOR THE TOPPING

2 to 3 tablespoons turbinado sugar (or other coarse sugar)

Preheat the oven to 375°F. Butter an 8 x 8-inch baking pan (you can also make this in a 9½-inch deep-dish pie pan). Set aside.

PREPARE THE PIECRUST: Remove 1 disk of the chilled pie dough from the refrigerator. Roll out the dough into a 12-inch circle on a lightly floured surface. Transfer the pastry dough to a large baking pan lined with baking parchment. Place the pan in the refrigerator to chill while preparing the filling.

PREPARE THE FILLING: Place the sliced fruits, arrowroot, sugar, crystallized ginger, and salt in a medium bowl. Stir together with a spoon until well combined. Cover the bowl with a kitchen cloth and leave to sit for 10 minutes.

ASSEMBLE THE PIE: Pour the fruit mixture into the prepared pan. Cover with the chilled pie dough, pinching the edges in. Beat the egg yolk and water together to create the egg wash. Using a pastry brush, brush the top of the crust with the egg wash.

Cut four to six 2-inch slits across the top of the dough, creating steam vents. Sprinkle the turbinado sugar across the surface of the pie. Bake for 35 to 40 minutes, until the crust is golden brown. Cool on a wire rack for at least 1 hour before serving.

CHOCOLATE CHERRY HAND PIES

Cherries enrobed in a buttery shell sound delectable. Add in a square of dark chocolate and things get even better. Make it small enough to fit in your hand and you've pretty much achieved the ideal dessert.

Makes a dozen hand pies

TO MAKE

PREPARE THE HAND PIE DOUGH CIRCLES: Remove 1 disk of chilled pie dough from the refrigerator. Roll it out into a 12- to 14-inch circle on a lightly floured surface.

FOR THE FILLING

1¼ pounds sweet cherries,

pitted and stemmed

¼ cup sugar

3 tablespoons arrowroot or

cornstarch

1 teaspoon almond extract

Pinch of sea salt

One 3-ounce dark choc-

olate bar

FOR THE EGG WASH

1 egg yolk

1 tablespoon whole milk

Using a 4-inch cookie cutter, cut out 12 rounds. Transfer the cut rounds to a baking parchment– or silicone mat–lined cookie sheet.

Repeat with the second disk of chilled pie dough. Refrigerate the prepped dough rounds while you prepare the filling.

PREPARE THE FILLING: Place the cherries, sugar, arrowroot, almond extract, and salt in a medium bowl. Stir together with a spoon until well combined. Mash the cherries gently with the back of the spoon to release their juices. Cover the bowl with a kitchen cloth and leave to sit for 15 minutes.

ASSEMBLE THE HAND PIES: Preheat the oven to 350°F. Remove the sheets of chilled dough rounds from the refrigerator. Mound about 5 to 6 cherries on top of each dough round on one cookie sheet, leaving about a ¼-inch border. Place a small bit of chocolate atop each mound of cherries.

Cover each cherry and chocolate mound with the remaining 12 dough rounds. Press the edges together with the tines of a fork to seal. Beat the egg yolk with the milk. Brush lightly over the top of each pie. Bake for 25 to 30 minutes, until the crusts are golden brown. Cool on a wire rack at least 30 minutes before serving.

Southern Comfort

Southern foods and summer were meant to go together. All that heat makes for an inspired kitchen, right? This gathering thanks chefs and growers alike for taking the heat and continuing to keep things growing and simmering when the mercury spikes.

THE HISTORY OF FOOD in the southeastern United States is a rich and diverse one. Native cultural practices long present in the area merged with the varied culinary traditions of the early colonialists, explorers, and African slaves, forging an incredible tapestry of flavors. A gathering celebrating these foods and food traditions will be as flavorful as it is fun. Expect offerings like "my mama's potato salad" (as detailed by one of my guests), deviled eggs rich with mayonnaise, and cold fried chicken. Get ready to hear stories about generationally bestowed family-secret recipes. Prepare to dance like a fool (literally) in a southern tradition, the cakewalk. Overall, know that a gathering focused on southern foods will leave you inspired, enriched, and very, very satiated.

I grew up in a home devoted at its very core to southern foods. There was always a canister of bacon drippings on the counter (meaning bacon was always also present). A large jar of Duke's mayonnaise was forever available in the refrigerator. Chicken and dumplings were placed on the dinner table with a high degree of frequency. Sweet tea was the beverage of choice. Biscuits and cornbread were in regular rotation. Ours was a kitchen full of the fat, sweetness, and soul of southern cuisine.

It was from my maternal grandmother, a southern woman from the top of her beauty parlor–styled hairdo to the souls of her red leather boots, that I learned my love of canning. Nanny and her second husband, Papa John, kept a large garden on their U-pick blueberry farm in Chesapeake, Virginia. In her kitchen, I learned about bread and butter pickles, grape jelly, and pressure-canned green beans. In her garden, I unearthed potatoes and gorged on vine-ripened tomatoes. And in her barn, I gathered eggs from her flock of chickens.

When I was twenty years old, I moved out of North Carolina to a large, metropolitan Northeast city on a whim. I didn't know anyone there and often found myself homesick. While I missed the people back home beyond words, it was often the flavors of North Carolina and its kitchens that called out their siren song to me the loudest. I missed biscuits and gravy. I missed country ham with red-eye gravy. I missed collards and black-eyed peas and hush puppies. Those foods weren't just the stuff of meals, they were friends, with memories and histories and stories packed with meaning and significance and milestones.

Not only does this gathering offer a chance for a southern foods feast, it suggests throwing another historical vestige of the southern states into the mix—the cakewalk. As your friends gather together and dance with winning conviction, the long summer night will shift from twilight to firefly hour, the sky from blue to pink, violet, and indigo. Southern foods comfort the belly and the soul. This exultation of all they have to offer will delight your guests, satisfy your hunger, and make the flavors of the South shine.

SETTING THE SCENE

A southern foods summer potluck should be all about languid, slow, stick-around-for-a-while comfort. It's going to be hot, it's going to be delicious, and it's going to be an absolute blast.

A PRETTY PICNIC: Ask each guest to bring a pretty picnic blanket. Spread them on the ground, either around low, communal tables or in a circle, so that guests can see one another, mingle, and keep the setting intimate.

CANDLELIGHT: I also asked guests to bring a mason jar with a candle inside. Vintage, modern, half-pint, pint, quart, and gallon jars are all welcome, as are tea lights, votives, and pillar candles. If you'll be eating at tables, set the jars and candles out there. Otherwise, adorn the feasting table with each guest's offerings.

COUNTRY CHIC: Growing up in the South as I did, the iconic red paisley handkerchief seemed to serve as the unofficial textile of the region. Paying homage to its ubiquitous presence, I sourced an inexpensive bundle of the cloths from the Internet and used them as napkins at the gathering. Everyone enjoyed the reference; guests who wanted a functional memento from the event took their handkerchief home to wash and use again.

BALLADS AND BLUES: For the cakewalk, you'll need some music. Since this gathering is all about the South, a hefty dose of country music's finest offerings is in order. If you or someone you know owns a portable record player (and some vinyl!), a bit of vintage flair would be fun. Otherwise, a playlist that includes a bit of Dolly Parton, Patsy Cline, Johnny Cash, and Merle Haggard will impart the perfect vibe.

No true southern-themed get-together would be complete without a cakewalk. Historically, cakewalks involve guests dancing in a numbered circle to music and then, when the music stops, landing on a number marked by either a placard or chalk (if the circle is marked out on the ground). A number is drawn, and the person on, or closest to, that number wins a cake provided by guests. Since not everyone may feel confident in their cake-baking skills, consider doing a "handmade" cakewalk. This riff on the original translates to everyone (or every family) bringing something handmade or homemade to give away.

If one of your guests makes a mean granola, they can bring a canister of that. If it's a jar of jam or pickles, or a batch of brownies or cookies, or a bar of soap, or a candle, or a jar of honey, encourage guests to bring those things. Alternately, if they're worried about their skill set, tell them to feel free to bring something handmade by someone else (e.g., purchased at the nearby farmers' market, local purveyor, etc.). When guests arrive, hide their offerings in paper bags so the gifts will be a surprise each time. Put a number on the front of each bag and, when the music stops and a number is selected, award the chosen bag to the guest in front of that numbered sign. Keep dancing (and removing already selected numbers and numbered signs after each walk) until every guest that participated in the handmade cakewalk has been given a gift.

YOU WILL NEED

- 4-foot wooden stakes (see Note)
- 1-inch-thick wood signs (see Note)
- Wood screws
- Paintbrushes
- Mixed paints
- Rubber mallet (for hammering the stakes into the ground)

Having the guests make the signs used in the cakewalk is a great way to both inspire creativity and send home guests with a memento. Simple wooden stakes are topped off with wood signs. As guests arrive, take their handmade gift, assign them a number, and then have them decorate their sign with that number in any way they see fit. Next, have them write their assigned number on a small piece of paper, which they'll then drop into a hat or basket. Those pieces of paper will correspond with the number written on the front of the bag containing the gift they brought. At the end of the cakewalk, guests can bring home the sign they decorated as a keepsake of the event.

Note: The number of wooden stakes and signs needed will be determined by the number of guests participating in the cakewalk. I typically assign each household one number/stake, but if individual members of a household bring their own gifts, then multiple numbers can be assigned.

TO MAKE

Take the wooden stakes (one end should be pointy) and screw 1-inch-thick square boards to the non-pointy ends. The squares can be whatever size you like. I cut the squares out of an 8-inch-wide board. It's best to attach the squares so that the top of the square is just below the top of the stake, so that the stake is easier to hammer into the ground.

Have guests paint the cakewalk signs as they arrive, following the instructions for numbering outlined above. After they are painted, hammer the stakes into the ground in a circle, using a blunt object such as a rubber mallet.

CAKEWALK

While the exact origin of the cakewalk is a contested subject, several theories abound. One theory maintains the cakewalk originated as a parody of the formal ballroom dancing preferred by white slave owners, resulting in satirical exaggerations of European dance moves. A competing theory holds the cakewalk developed in the state of Florida, as a sort of pantomime of the war dances of the Seminole natives. Slaves living in the area were spectators at a number of these dances, which involved exaggerated gesturing and movements alternating with slow-moving coupled processions. Either way, the cakewalk's association with southern culture is a rich, interwoven one. Incorporating it into a gathering celebrating all the best the South has to offer will make the event one that is long remembered, well after the music stops and the guests have made their way home.

Oh, the options when it comes to a southern foods gathering. You might find it more challenging to whittle down your choices than to come up with them in the first place! The offerings are vast, the flavors varied, and the cuisines to draw upon distinct. From low-country shrimp and grits to bayou gumbo, southern cuisine moves from coastal waters to piedmont grain fields to mountaintop apple orchards. Whatever you choose, it's bound to be tasty!

MENU SUGGESTIONS

Collard Green Galette*, Pimento Cheese Dip*, Bourbon Iced Tea*, Peach Sonker*,
Basil Deviled Eggs, Cold Fried Chicken, Bourbon-Soaked Watermelon Bites,
Spicy Cheese Straws, Dilly Coleslaw, Banana Pudding, Sugar-Glazed Ham,
Blueberry Corn Muffins, Chicken and Dumplings, Boiled Peanuts

COLLARD GREEN GALETTE

No southern foods gathering would be complete without collards on the menu. In this recipe, I cook them down with crumbled bacon, heap the greens into a pastry dough circle, cut the baked galette into wedges, and serve each piece with a spicy apple cider vinegar. These greens are sure to please culinary traditionalists and radicals alike!

Serves 6 to 8

YOU WILL NEED

½ recipe Basic Pie Dough (page 17)

FOR THE SEASONED VINEGAR

1 cup apple cider vinegar

2 tablespoons sugar

Pinch of sea salt

A couple grinds of black pepper

Pinch of hot pepper flakes, or to taste

FOR THE COLLARD FILLING

5 slices of bacon

1 sweet onion, sliced

2 cloves garlic, minced

1 large bowl of chopped collard greens

4 cups chicken stock

½ cup white or rosé wine

¼ cup white wine vinegar

2 to 3 tablespoons cornmeal (for the galette crust)

FOR THE EGG WASH

1 egg yolk

1 tablespoon cold water

TO MAKE

PREPARE THE CRUST: Remove 1 disk of the chilled pie dough from the refrigerator. Roll out the dough into a 12-inch circle on a lightly floured surface. Transfer the pastry dough to a large baking pan lined with baking parchment. Place the pan in the refrigerator to chill while you prepare the filling.

PREPARE THE SEASONED VINEGAR: Warm the vinegar in a small saucepan over low heat until hot to the touch. Remove from heat. Add the sugar and stir until it has fully dissolved. Add the remaining ingredients and stir to combine. Set aside to cool. Once the vinegar reaches room temperature, transfer to a spouted container and set aside to serve with the galette.

PREPARE THE FILLING: In a large stockpot over medium-high heat, cook the bacon until it starts to get a little crispy. Remove the bacon, place it on a paper towel set onto a plate, and set the plate aside. Cook the onion in the bacon fat for about 10 minutes, until it begins to brown around the edges. Add the garlic and cook for 1 more minute. Add the collard greens and cook, stirring often, for 3 to 4 minutes, until the greens begin to wilt. Crumble the bacon into the greens and stir to fully incorporate. Add the rest of the ingredients and reduce the heat to medium-low. Cook, stirring occasionally, for about 1 hour, until the cooking liquid has evaporated from the bottom of the pan. Transfer the greens to a bowl to cool for at least 10 minutes. While the greens cool, preheat the oven to 375°F.

ASSEMBLE THE GALETTE: Mound the greens mixture in the middle of the chilled pie dough. Gently press the mixture toward the edge of the pastry, leaving a 2-inch border all around. Fold up the border, overlapping the pie dough and pressing folds together every few inches.

Beat the egg yolk with the water. Brush the folded crust edges with the egg wash. Sprinkle the crust edges with the cornmeal. Bake the galette for 35 to 40 minutes, until the crust is golden. Cool on a wire rack for at least 15 to 20 minutes before serving; serve with the seasoned vinegar.

PIMENTO CHEESE DIP

My maternal grandmother was a huge fan of hoop cheese. A farmer's cheese made from curds drained of all their whey and then pressed into a round mold, hoop cheese used to be *the* cheese of the South. It's harder to come by these days, owing in

part to its short shelf life. If you can't find it, you can use a mild cheddar cheese instead.

Makes 3 cups

TO MAKE

In a food processor, combine the cheese, mayonnaise, relish, paprika, and hot sauce and process until smooth. Add the chopped pimento and process just until the pepper pieces are incorporated but not fully pureed. Transfer the cheese mixture to a serving bowl and top with the diced pimento.

YOU WILL NEED

2 pounds hoop cheese (or cheddar cheese), cubed

1 cup mayonnaise

½ cup relish (green tomato or sweet pickle)

1 tablespoon smoked paprika

A couple dashes of hot sauce

½ cup chopped pimento

1 to 2 tablespoons diced pimento (for topping the dip)

Iced tea holds prominence in the pantheon of south-ern beverages. Bourbon (and probably moonshine!) comes in at a very close second, however, so partner-ing the two seemed like a marriage made in southern heaven. Add a slice of fresh peach and a sprig of mint and you've got one of the most iconic (and delicious) blends imaginable.

Makes about 1½ gallons

YOU WILL NEED

- 4 cups water (for simple syrup)
- 2 cups sugar
- 4 cups cold water (to cool the simple syrup)
- 8 cups strong black tea, cooled
- 4 cups bourbon
- Juice of 6 lemons
- 4 cups ice, plus more to serve
- A peach wedge and a mint leaf for each glass

TO MAKE

Warm 4 cups of water in a medium pot over medium-low heat until hot to the touch. Mix in the sugar and stir until fully dissolved. Add 4 cups of cold water to the simple syrup. Stir to fully combine.

Mix the cooled simple syrup and steeped tea in a large container. Add the bourbon, lemon juice, and ice; stir to combine. Serve in ½-pint mason jars, over ice, with a peach wedge and a mint leaf in each glass.

PEACH SONKER

The "sonker" is a type of deep-dish cobbler-like pie native to North Carolina, the state in which I live. It makes use of whatever fruit is abundant and in season at the time of baking; in this case, that's peaches. Historically, these types of pie are baked in large quantities to feed all of the workers on a farm. If you'd like to make a larger quantity, simply double all of the ingredient amounts and bake in a 9 x 13-inch baking pan.

Makes one 10-inch skillet pie

TO MAKE

PREPARE THE FILLING: Combine the peaches, sugar, arrowroot, flour, and cinnamon in a medium bowl. Stir until the ingredients are fully combined and the peach slices are well coated. Cover the bowl with a kitchen cloth and set aside for 15 minutes. Meanwhile, prepare the biscuit topping.

PREPARE THE BISCUIT TOPPING: Combine the flour, baking powder, baking soda, and salt in a medium bowl. Using a pastry cutter or fork, cut the butter cubes in until the mixture is crumbly and the butter is pea-size or smaller. Create a well in the center of the mixture. Pour in the buttermilk.

YOU WILL NEED

FOR THE FILLING

- 4 cups peaches (peeled, pitted, and cut into ¼-inch slices)
- 1 cup sugar
- ¼ cup arrowroot or cornstarch
- 2 tablespoons all-purpose flour
- 1 teaspoon ground cinnamon
- 3 tablespoons unsalted butter, melted

FOR THE BISCUIT TOPPING

- 1 cup all-purpose flour
- 1 teaspoon baking powder
- ¼ teaspoon baking soda
- ¼ teaspoon sea salt
- 3 tablespoons unsalted butter, cubed
- ¾ cup buttermilk

Using a mixing spoon, gently incorporate the milk just until all of the dry ingredients are moistened. The mixture will look quite wet at this point, but that's fine.

ASSEMBLE THE SONKER: Preheat the oven to 425°F.

Butter a 10-inch skillet or a 9-inch pie pan. Place the peach mixture into the prepared skillet. Using a spoon, dollop the surface of the peaches with the biscuit topping, aiming for 3-tablespoon mounds. You needn't be terribly specific on the biscuit amounts; as long as the surface is dotted with small-size biscuit mounds, you're in good shape. Pour the melted butter over the biscuit topping.

Bake for 15 minutes, then reduce the oven temperature to 350°F and continue baking for an additional 30 minutes, until the filling is bubbly and the biscuit tops are golden brown. Cool on a wire rack for at least 30 minutes before serving.

Ice Cream Social

When it's hot and humid, ice cream is the order of the day. You won't have a hard time . recruiting your nearest and dearest to this party! Celebrate the frozen, sweet splendor that makes the dog days of summer a bit more hospitable.

I CAN THINK OF FEW FOODS more iconic and representative of summer than ice cream. Barbecue, lemonade, and fruit pies nip closely at the heels for second-place status, but it's ice cream, with its trifecta delivery of sweet, creamy, and cold (the real deal clincher) that makes the frozen dessert such a seasonal favorite. Children and seniors alike would gladly welcome a scoop or two on a hot summer day (oftentimes in lieu of a proper meal!). An ice cream social is a perfect opportunity to gather your nearest and dearest for a sweet-filled afternoon, full of flavor, fun, and frozen goodness!

I grew up in an ice-cream-loving family. My maternal grandmother in particular couldn't get enough of the stuff. To this day, she'll scrimp on her dinner, pushing the food on her plate around and announcing to anyone listening that she couldn't possibly eat another thing, only to then suggest we have a hearty bowl of peach ice cream for dessert. She loves ice cream so much, in fact, that she tried to sneak tastes of it to my son when he was just a wee baby, before he'd even had any solid food whatsoever.

When I was a child, my mother, brother, and I lived for several years in Chesapeake and Virginia Beach, Virginia. My grandmother and her second husband were living there at the time as well. Summertime and autumn visits out to Nanny's farm inevitably concluded at Bergey's Dairy. Whether it was a scoop of fresh strawberry ice cream on a waffle cone or a generous bowlful of pumpkin ice cream (my absolute favorite), my brother and I treasured those times at Bergey's. We'd collect our treats, secure a seat outside the ice cream parlor, and take in the sights, sounds, and, yes, smells afforded by a working dairy farm.

The concept of an ice cream social as a means of entertainment developed in the United States in the nineteenth century. French confectioners, upon relocating to the United States after the French Revolution, began producing ice cream for the public in landscaped outdoor settings known as "ice cream gardens." Since women, female youth, and children at the time were prohibited from frequenting the taverns and pubs males enjoyed, ice cream gardens became popular locations for the well-to-do to socialize. These gardens, which often provided musical entertainment, fresh beverages, and light refreshments in addition to ice cream, were ideal spots for children to play, teenagers to flirt, and women to while away a hot summer's day.

As commercially produced ice cream gained in production scale, the cost of its manufacture went down. Accordingly, ice cream became more affordable and ice cream gardens as an elite socializing location became less common. The concept of an ice cream social was then appropriated by churches, typically in the form of fundraising events. Nowadays, ice cream socials are employed by a wide demographic, from churches to community groups to neighborhood block parties. This sort of party is a great means of mixing generations together too. At the gathering I hosted, all ages were accounted for, from babies not yet a year old on up through those with graying temples. Everyone was scooping, sprinkling, licking, and laughing, whether they had teeth or not! No matter the setting or the age, the outcome is always the same—smiling faces and full bellies.

SETTING THE SCENE

When it comes to an ice cream social, the vibe you're going for can be summed up in just one word—fun! From the icy sweet eats to the colorful décor, this gathering invites your inner child to grab a cone or a spoon and giggle with happiness.

BOWLS, SPOONS, AND CONES: Frozen scoops of ice cream need somewhere to go, so having plenty of bowls, spoons, and cones on hand is a must. If you fear you won't have enough for everyone, ask guests to bring along a bowl and spoon for each person in their party.

RIBBON BANNER: A decorative ribbon banner injects a bit of childlike whimsy into the gathering. Ask guests to bring a bit of ribbon with them, corresponding to whatever ice cream or topping they've selected (e.g., brown ribbon for chocolate

ice cream, mauve ribbon for raspberry sorbet). It can be on a spool or already cut to length but should be at least 2 feet long. As they arrive, have the guests attach their ribbon to some twine or rope secured in advance of the event behind the feasting table. When the social concludes, they can either take their ribbon with them or leave it as a gift to the host.

ICE, ICE BABY: All of that ice cream needs to remain frozen for the duration of the party, and readily accessible at the same time. The solution? A galvanized tub or cooler filled with ice. You'll likely be busy with finalizing last-minute party details, so ask a guest to pick up several bags of ice on the way.

GET THE SCOOP: Unless you own an ice cream store, it's unlikely you'll have enough scoops of your own available. Ask guests to bring a scoop with their ice cream, making sure they collect it when they depart.

SHARE AN ICY MEMORY

Many people have vivid memories surrounding ice cream. Maybe it was a dairy farm they used to frequent as a child (like me!), or eating ice cream with a beloved grandparent, or summers spent seaside eating ice cream on a boardwalk during family reunions. Once guests are settled down with their bowls or cones, ask them to share any treasured recollections related to ice cream.

HANDMADE PINWHEELS

Few crafts say summertime fun more to me than pinwheels. Spinning in a warm, gentle breeze, a kaleidoscope of patterns and colors, they invite whimsy, laughter, and silliness, all traits most welcome at an ice cream social. If children are making these, be certain to have an adult supervising, as scissors and pushpins are involved.

TO MAKE

Fold a paper square diagonally, corner to corner, pressing hard to form creases in the paper. Unfold and repeat with the opposite corners. Using the scissors, carefully cut into the fold lines, stopping about halfway along each crease. Gather every other corner, pulling it toward the center of the paper.

Pierce the tips of the gathered corners of paper with a pushpin, taking care to go through all 4 layers of paper while not sticking yourself with the pin. Push the pin, with the 4 corners attached, through the center of the paper. Holding onto the pushpin and paper with one hand, use your other hand to push the pin through the eraser end of the pencil.

YOU WILL NEED

- 6 x 6-inch squares of decorative paper (see Note)
- Scissors
- Pushpins
- Eraser-ended pencils

Note: I used precut squares of patterned scrapbook paper for making my pinwheels, as I found them to be the perfect size. You could also use handmade papers; simply cut each piece to the dimensions suggested above.

COOKING IT UP

An ice cream social is an incredible opportunity to get creative with your sweet tooth. From homemade ice cream to crunchy nut toppings, chocolate shavings, and marshmallow fluff, this is the ideal showcase for every sweet delectable imaginable. Ask each guest to bring a pint of ice cream (homemade, locally made, store-bought, it's all welcome!), along with a topping. It might be good to get a sense of what everyone is bringing in advance, so as to avoid being inundated with only chocolate ice cream and caramel sauce.

MENU SUGGESTIONS

Blackberry Mint Ice Cream*, Boozy Maraschino Cherries*, Sugar and Spice Nuts*, Orange Caramel Sauce*, Homemade Marshmallow Fluff, Pineapple with Fresh Mint, Strawberry Balsamic Ice Cream, Rum Caramel Sauce, Peach Praline Ice Cream, Cocoa Nibs, Stout Beer Brownies, Chocolate Chocolate Chip Ice Cream, Crumbled Shortbread, Maple Syrup Wet Nuts

BLACKBERRY MINT ICE CREAM

Homemade ice cream is such a treat. Not only is it fun to make; it's nice to be able to customize flavor options to your exact preferences and those of your family. Here I've combined hot-weather favorite mint ice cream with fresh, seasonal blackberries. The end result is cool, creamy, and beautiful!

Makes 5 cups

TO MAKE

Whisk the sugar and eggs together in a large bowl until the mixture thickens slightly. Add the arrowroot and whisk until fully incorporated. Set the bowl aside.

Warm the half-and-half in a heavy-bottom saucepan over medium heat. When it reaches a gentle simmer, slowly, carefully whisk it into the egg and sugar mixture. Return the mixture to the saucepan. Cook over low heat, stirring continually, until the mixture thickens slightly and clings to the back of a spoon. Remove from heat. Strain the custard through a fine-mesh sieve into a medium bowl. Set aside to cool for 1 hour.

YOU WILL NEED

- 1 cup sugar
- 2 large eggs
- 1½ tablespoons arrowroot or cornstarch
- 2 cups half-and-half
- 2 cups heavy cream
- ¼ cup fresh mint leaves
- ¼ teaspoon mint extract
- 1 pint fresh blackberries

Stir in the heavy cream, fresh mint, and mint extract. Cover the bowl with a kitchen cloth or overturned plate and refrigerate for at least 4 hours or overnight. Whisk the chilled mixture, then strain off the fresh mint and either discard or compost it.

Transfer the mixture to an ice cream maker. Freeze it according to your machine's instructions, adding the blackberries once the mixture begins to thicken and firm up, 10 to 15 minutes into processing time.

BOOZY MARASCHINO CHERRIES

I've been a fan of maraschino cherries in my ice cream for as long as I can remember. Now that I'm old enough to know about the artificial dyes used in many commercially prepared options, I decided that, like many things in the culinary realm, home-made is best! So that kiddos and adults can enjoy these cherries alike, I've included a tip for making them alcohol-free.

Makes 4 cups

YOU WILL NEED

1½ pounds sweet cherries, such as Bing

¾ cup sugar

¾ cup water

1 teaspoon sea salt

Juice from 1 lemon

1½ cups cherry liqueur (see Note)

1 cup pomegranate juice

TO MAKE

Wash the cherries in cold water. Using either a cherry pitter or a paring knife, pit the cherries. I like to leave the stems on for decorative effect. Simply angle the pitter or knife slightly off to one side in order to remove the pit but leave the stem intact.

In a medium saucepan, combine the sugar, water, and salt. Bring to a gentle simmer over medium-low heat, stirring to dissolve the sugar completely. Remove the pan from heat and stir in the lemon juice, cherry liqueur, and pomegranate juice. Place the cherries in a heatproof jar. Pour the cherry liquid over them. Cover with a lid, allow the jar to cool to room temperature, and serve. Refrigerate any unused portion and use within 1 month.

Note: I used Luxardo brand cherry liqueur. To make this alcohol-free, replace the cherry liqueur with 1½ cups water mixed with 2 teaspoons almond extract.

SUGAR AND SPICE NUTS

YOU WILL NEED

1   pound mixed nuts

2   tablespoons unsalted
    butter

¼   cup sugar

1   teaspoon sea salt

1   teaspoon ground cinna-
    mon

1   teaspoon ground nutmeg

½   teaspoon ground allspice

My husband is a fan of mixing up textures in the kitchen. If he's having ice cream, its smooth, deliciousness isn't enough for him—he wants some crunch with it too! Here's our solution—sweet, spicy chopped nuts. These are easy to make and have proven to be a perennial ice cream social crowd pleaser.

Makes 2 cups

TO MAKE

Crush the nuts by pulsing them in a food processor or pounding them under a dish towel with a heavy pan. Sift the nut dust through a strainer, reserving the crushed nuts.

Toast the nuts in a dry skillet over medium heat for 3 to 4 minutes. Add the butter. Stir until melted and thoroughly blended into the nut mixture. Stir in the sugar, salt, and spices. Remove from the heat.

Spread the mixture out on a cookie sheet to cool. Refrigerate any unused portion and eat within 1 month.

ORANGE CARAMEL SAUCE

While caramel sauce on its own is a glorious thing, sweetening the deal with a hint of orange makes it truly transcendent. When melting the sugar, watch it carefully. You want it to take on the patina of an aged copper penny, a trick I learned from food writer and dessert expert David Lebovitz. Don't rush to melt it too fast; medium-low heat and a watchful eye will get it to just the right shade, texture, and, ultimately, flavor.

Makes 2 cups

TO MAKE

Melt the sugar in a high-sided, heavy-bottom pot over medium-low heat until it turns the color of an old copper penny. Remove the pan from heat and carefully add the orange juice, taking care not to scald yourself on the steam it produces.

Return the pan to the stovetop. Warm it over low heat for 3 minutes, stirring occasionally. Add the remaining ingredients; simmer for 10 to 15 minutes, until the sauce turns syrupy. Remove the pan from heat. Transfer the sauce to a heatproof container. Allow it to cool slightly before serving.

YOU WILL NEED

2 cups sugar

½ cup orange juice

½ cup heavy cream

2 tablespoons unsalted butter

2 teaspoons vanilla extract

1 teaspoon orange extract

½ ounce orange liqueur (optional)

In a Pickle

On those days of summer when the garden's bounty threatens to overwhelm, turn to pickling. This party makes short work of the task at hand, bottling up all that goodness.

I LOVE LATE SUMMER. It's the most scandalous time of the year, at least, that is, in the garden. Farmers' markets, backyard gardens, and just about every plot and container planted with seeds and watered with love are heaving and bursting forth with a cornucopia of offerings. From fruitful, lush watermelons to bountiful zucchini, verdant cucumbers to slinky okra fingers, the harvest of seasonal fruits and vegetables is definitely upon us. After you've eaten as much as you can fresh, frozen some, and perhaps even given a bit away (I'm looking at you, zucchini!), it's time to bring out the canner and fill some jars with pickles. A pickling party brings to life the saying "many hands make light work." You get help preserving the harvest, your guests leave with a bottled treat, and the growing efforts of all of those fruits and vegetables gets honored in the process.

I had the immense fortune of growing up with a grandmother skilled in the art and craft of home canning. Nanny was an avid canner in my early childhood, putting up jar after jar of beans, corns, bread and butter pickles, tomatoes, and more come summertime. Her simmering pots and steaming kitchen were a wonderland to me, full of mystique. I'd stand close to her as she worked, gazing curiously as she'd pour ladles full of brine over pickles and secure screw bands atop the lids, knowing by feel just when she'd reached the right degree of tightness. Her kitchen smelled of vinegar and sugar and sounded like a low-key jazz band composed of bubbling pots, rattling lids, and simmering saucepans.

It was years before I'd "take to the jar" myself. I'd always think of Nanny and her summertime canning and pickling sessions whenever I'd see a bounty of produce, though. As I entered my early thirties, the lure of canning and my heritage of it called to me like a culinary siren song, beckoning me to fire up the canner and store food away in jars. I thought I'd start easy, with some strawberry jam. That first foray into the wide world of home canning was a kind of Pandora's box awakening for me. Suddenly, every tomato, cucumber, pepper, or blackberry was destined in my mind's eye for some pint of this, some quart of that.

Now, as an experienced home canner who loves the endeavor so much I've even penned a book on the topic, I've learned to temper my enthusiasm when greeted with a bushel of green beans or a peck of apples. Over the years of bottling all manner of canned goods, I've surmised we're more apt, as a household, to eat quarts of straight-up, classic dill pickles than pints of fennel relish (tasty though it may be!). I've realized it's better to make peach lavender butter with fresh peaches than to can them as halves and that plums are more likely to be consumed if they are cooked with sugar and lemon verbena into an herbaceous jam than simply placed in jars with whole cinnamon sticks.

My experiences in canning have left me with more than just a well-stocked pantry. They've taught me about temperance, and patience, and taking the time to do something with deliberation and intention and thoughtfulness. When you put fruits and vegetables in jars, nestling them in with herbs, spices, and flavorings of every persuasion, you're putting time in a bottle, capturing a smell, a feel, and a flavor that is so very "right now." At this gathering, held on my patio one balmy August day, my friends and I preserved laughter, camaraderie, and, yes, vegetables. We worked hard, ate heartily afterward, and left with more than just a jar of pickles. I thank my grandmother for teaching me, so very long ago, that saving the harvest is good for the pantry, for the garden, and, perhaps most important, for the human soul.

This gathering is all about sharing the workload while having a good time. If you find yourself, or your guests, whistling while you work, consider your goal to have been achieved!

TAKE THE CANNING OUT OF THE KITCHEN: I often head outdoors when pickling, literally taking some of the heat out of the kitchen. With an extension cord and some portable burners, you can make your pickles while keeping your cool!

MASON JAR HERB POTS: Decorating the event with herbs typically used in home canning is a great way to enliven a table with fresh greenery. Ask guests to bring a potted herb often used in pickling such as basil, oregano, thyme, mint, or dill. When they arrive, transfer the herbs into canning jars (either modern or vintage) and fill them with potting soil. As the guests depart, they can choose to either take their herb home with them or leave it with the host for potting.

A PICKLED PALETTE: For this gathering, I wanted to invoke the green shades of produce typically used in pickling (think cucumbers, okra, and green beans), as well as the gentle browns of pickling spices, such as cinnamon, cloves, mustard seeds, and allspice. Linens and tableware in this color scheme are a perfect complement to the pickling party, as well as the summertime landscape itself.

MAKE PICKLES

Making pickles, while a wonderful kitchen craft, can be time consuming, given all the washing, chopping, and other prep work that's involved. What better way, then, to put up summer pantry provisions than by gathering your nearest and dearest to share the bushels of ripening beans and cukes? Ask friends to pitch in, either by bringing some of the necessities for canning (electric cords, burners, jars, lids, screw bands, canner, etc.) or some of the produce, herbs, spices, and vinegar you'll be using.

YOU WILL NEED

- Several fresh okra pods
- Toothpicks
- Assorted craft paints
- Painter's palette (plastic or wooden)
- Scraps of paper
- Gift tags (with hole cut-outs)
- Jute, sisal, twine, or raffia

One of the best things about canning is that you're creating not just a pantry full of provisions for yourself and your family, but that you're making ready-in-a-dash gifts as well. A jar of spicy and herbaceous pickled okra is a wonderful item to give as a housewarming, birthday, holiday, or any-occasion gift. Making okra-stamped gift tags the day of your pickling party imparts a bit of whimsical yet referential decorative presentation.

TO MAKE

Slice off the stem portion on several okra pods. Place a toothpick vertically through the okra pod's top. This helps you to gain a better grasp when putting the okra into the paint in the upcoming steps. Using a pointy-tipped knife, carefully remove a few of the seeds

inside each prepared pod (this helps to achieve a clearer, more detailed print upon stamping).

Guests can choose whichever paint color they'd like to stamp and place a small amount of it into the painter's palette. Grasp an okra pod using the inserted tooth-pick for support and dip it into your chosen paint color. Stamp the paint-covered pod onto a piece of scrap paper to remove any excess paint.

Next, write the name of whatever you're gifting on one side of the gift tag. Then stamp the okra pod onto the other side of the gift tag in a decorative motif. Once the tag has dried, thread a bit of jute, sisal, twine, or raffia through the gift tag's hole and affix it to your jar.

At its core, a pickling party is all about, well, the pickles! After making up a batch (or two, depending on the size of your crowd) and creating decorative gift tags, gather guests to feast on a modern incarnation of the traditional ploughman's lunch. Cheeses, spreads, pickles (of course!), charcuterie, breads, and crisp beers are the order of the day. Here are three recipes for pickling up some of summer's most bountiful vegetables: okra, green beans, and cucumbers.

MENU SUGGESTIONS

Moroccan Road Pickled Okra*, Caliente Green Beans*, Herbes de Provence Pickled Cucumbers*,

Aged cheddar cheeses, Salumi and prosciutto, Sourdough bread loaves and baguettes,

Goat cheese, Muscadine, Scuppernong, and Concord grapes, Cherry tomatoes,

Assorted homemade jams and preserves, Bread and butter pickles, Fresh or dried figs,

Infused honey, Hard cider and wheat beers

MOROCCAN ROAD PICKLED OKRA

I love it when foods combine fresh herbs and spices, all in one dish. This is my homage to all things Moroccan, a cuisine incredibly skilled at the mixture of the two. These jars look truly stunning, making them ideal options for gift giving (if you possess the self-restraint not to munch on them all yourself first!).

Makes five 1-pint jars

TO MAKE

Sterilize five 1-pint mason jars, lids, and screw rings. Place the jars in a canner or large stockpot filled with water and set over medium-high heat. Bring just to the boiling point, turn off the heat, and set aside. Place the lids and screw rings in a small saucepan, fill with water, bring to a boil, turn off the heat, and set aside.

Wash the okra and trim the stem end, taking caution to not pierce the pod. Set aside. In a medium stainless-steel saucepan, combine the vinegar, water, and salt. This is your pickling brine. Bring to a boil, cover, and remove from the heat.

YOU WILL NEED

  2 pounds okra (ideally, pods should be no longer than 4 inches long)
2½ cups white vinegar
2½ cups water
  ¼ cup pickling or kosher salt
  5 cloves garlic, peeled (1 clove per jar)
  5 cinnamon sticks (1 stick per jar)
  5 teaspoons coriander seeds (1 teaspoon per jar)
  5 teaspoons cumin seeds (1 teaspoon per jar)
 10 springs fresh mint (2 sprigs per jar)

Place the hot jars on top of a kitchen cloth on the counter. Into each jar, place: 1 peeled garlic clove, 1 cinnamon stick, 1 teaspoon coriander seeds, 1 teaspoon cumin seeds, and 2 sprigs fresh mint. Pack the okra upright into jars; fill the jars snugly but not too tightly. With the help of a canning funnel, ladle the pickling brine over the okra, reserving ½-inch headspace. Use a nonmetallic spatula to remove any trapped air bubbles, and wipe the rims clean with a damp cloth.

Place on the lids and screw bands, tightening only until fingertip-tight. Using a jar lifter, place the jars in the canner. Process for 10 minutes in a boiling-water bath. Remember to adjust for altitude. Store in a cool location out of direct sunlight and consume within 1 year.

CALIENTE GREEN BEANS

A bit of heat and spice is the perfect foil for the sweet crunch of green beans. These taste best after they've had some time in the jar, so let them age at least 2 weeks before opening. Though delicious on their own, they're wonderful partnered with a barbecue sandwich or a chunk of mild cheddar.

Makes five 1-pint jars

YOU WILL NEED

- 2 pounds green beans
- 2½ cups white vinegar
- 2½ cups water
- ¼ cup pickling or kosher salt
- 5 cloves garlic, sliced (1 clove per jar)
- 2½ teaspoons hot pepper flakes (½ teaspoon per jar)
- 5 teaspoons brown mustard seeds (1 teaspoon per jar)
- 2½ teaspoons smoked paprika (½ teaspoon per jar)

TO MAKE

Sterilize five 1-pint mason jars, lids, and screw rings. Place the jars in a canner or large stockpot filled with water and set over medium-high heat. Bring just to the boiling point, turn off the heat, and set aside. Place the lids and screw rings in a small saucepan, fill with water, bring to a boil, turn off the heat, and set aside.

Wash the green beans and trim the ends. Set aside.

In a medium stainless-steel saucepan, combine the vinegar, water, and salt. This is your pickling brine. Bring to a boil, cover, and remove from heat.

Place the hot jars on top of a kitchen cloth on the counter. Into each jar, place: 1 sliced garlic clove, ½ teaspoon hot pepper flakes, 1 teaspoon brown mustard seeds, and ½ teaspoon smoked paprika. Pack the green beans upright into the jars; fill the jars snugly but not too tightly. With the help of a canning funnel, ladle the pickling brine over the beans, reserving ½-inch headspace. Use a nonmetallic spatula to remove any trapped air bubbles, and wipe the rims clean with a damp cloth.

Place on the lids and screw bands, tightening only until fingertip-tight. Using a jar lifter, place the jars in the canner. Process for 10 minutes in a boiling-water bath. Remember to adjust for altitude. Store in a cool location out of direct sunlight and use within 1 year.

HERBES DE PROVENCE PICKLED CUCUMBERS

On our honeymoon, my husband and I began with a five-night stay in Paris, before traveling by train to spend four nights in Monte Carlo and then, after that, three nights in Rome. It was, hand's down, the most wonderful vacation of my life (as it should be!). Though I don't recall the specific setting, somewhere during our time in France we had the Provençal herb blend herbes de Provence. Though the individual ingredients and proportions may vary from one producer to another, the blend is typically a mixture of oregano, thyme, savory, rosemary, sage, basil, and lavender. I adore it and figured it would make a perfect partner to pickles, which it does.

Makes eight 1-pint jars

YOU WILL NEED

- 6 pounds pickling cucumbers
- ¾ cup pickling salt
- 4 cups white vinegar
- 3½ cups water
- 8 tablespoons dried herbes de Provence (1 tablespoon per jar)

TO MAKE

Rinse the cucumbers in cold water. Scrub gently with a vegetable brush to loosen any hidden soil. Remove a thin slice from the blossom end of each cucumber (if you can't tell which end is the blossom end, just take a thin slice off of each end). Place the cucumbers in a nonreactive bowl, add ½ cup of the pickling salt, cover with water, place a plate or towel over the top, and set in a cool place or the refrigerator for at least 8 hours or overnight. Drain off the brining solution. Rinse the cucumbers thoroughly to remove the salt residue. Cut into halves or quarters. Set aside.

Sterilize eight 1-pint jars, lids, and screw rings. Place the jars in a canner or large stockpot filled with water and set over medium-high heat. Bring just to the boiling point, turn off the heat, and set aside. Place the lids and screw rings in a small saucepan, fill with water, bring to a boil, turn off the heat, and set aside.

In a medium stainless-steel pan, combine the vinegar, water, and remaining ¼

cup pickling salt. Bring to a boil and simmer for 5 minutes. Remove from the heat
and set aside.

Into each sterilized jar, place 1 tablespoon herbes de Provence. Pack the cucumbers into each jar and cover with the vinegar solution. Leave ½-inch headspace. Use
a nonmetallic spatula to remove any trapped air bubbles, and wipe the rims clean
with a damp cloth.

Place on the lids and screw bands, tightening only until fingertip-tight. Using a
jar lifter, place the jars in the canner. Process for 10 minutes in a boiling-water bath.
Remember to adjust for altitude. Store in a cool location out of direct sunlight and
use within one year.

AUTUMN

To Market, to Make It

The transition from summer to autumn is a bountiful one in the garden and at the market. This child-centric gathering celebrates the best of both seasons with each delicious bite.

FARMERS' MARKETS are little temporary utopias to me. Whenever I happen upon one, no matter if I'm in California, Paris, or a small town in the mountains of western North Carolina, I always find myself suddenly flooded with joy. The stacks of beets and lettuces and tomatoes, expertly arranged in woven baskets and wooden boxes, are so very lovely. The jars of honey and bars of beeswax for sale by local beekeepers are so captivating and beautiful. But it might just be the sight of children that enlivens me the most. Whenever I see a child at the market, I know that goodness is growing in their lives. A gathering based around children exploring farmers' markets and backyard gardens is one rife with fun, and destined to fill your guests with abundant joy themselves.

When I was twenty years old, I left the small southern town I was living in and headed north. Without knowing a soul there, I decided to move to Washington, D.C. I've always been bold and a bit fearlessly (or naively, depending on who you ask) brave. Moving to the "big city" felt like no big deal to me as I packed my things, kissed friends and family good-bye, and set my compass north.

After settling into a studio apartment my father's wife owned, I set out daily on walks around my new stomping grounds. I found the nearest grocer, located my neighborhood's post office, and decided on which coffee shop would become "mine." At first, it was bliss. I was young and unattached and inquisitive. I drank in my new city with thirst, almost to the point of intoxication. There were incredible (and free!) art and history museums. There were exotic foreign food stores. There were cultural celebrations and folks from all walks of life passing by me on the sidewalk. I was utterly and wholeheartedly smitten.

In the beginning, everything was great. But then the tide gradually began to shift. What started as an intrepid foray into a new landscape came to feel like a seismic rift that had lifted me far, far from home. I missed my friends and family. I missed southern accents, with their long drawls and extra syllables. I missed grits. I was alone in a strange place populated by strange people. I had no community, no roots. Where were "my people"? As it turned out, they were at the farmers' market.

I saw a flyer at a nearby natural foods store about a weekend farmers' market. As an avid lover of fresh produce and open-air markets, I knew I'd have to check it out. The next Saturday, I rode the subway out to the location detailed in the flyer. As I took the escalator out of the subterranean darkness, emerging into a cloudless blue sky that morning, something clicked. Not quite sure of what it was, I walked out of the station right into the market, set up along the sidewalk.

A saxophonist was standing off to one side of the market, passionately breathing soul and sound into the morning. Children walked by, one hand holding tight to Mom or Dad, the other grasping a bouquet of screaming yellow sunflowers. The smell of hot coffee and cinnamon buns permeated the place. And then it happened. Smiles. Anonymous, kind, knowing smiles showed up on the lips of strangers. They smiled at me just for being there, for sharing together this medley of abundance and nutrition and connection with soil and sky. I smiled in return and knew I'd found my tribe.

Farmers' markets are fantastic places to bring children to. Their curiosity is ignited, their senses stimulated, and, if a bakery selling stellar cinnamon buns is on hand, their bellies are happily filled. My son adores farmers' markets, running from booth to booth, grabbing an eggplant here, nibbling a cheese sample there. At this gathering, culinary pride was evident in both the children and their parents as they described what they had made together. Clearly, good times had been had at the market and in the kitchen alike. And when the paint came out and the crafting component of the party began, that happiness was magnified tenfold.

This gathering, focused on opening the dialogue of food and growing and soil and sky and community, is such a vital one to have with the little people in our lives. If you have no children, grab a niece or nephew or neighbor's child, pick up a market basket, and get ready to explore the world of fruits, vegetables, breads, jams, honey, flowers, and more with fresh, youthful eyes.

SETTING THE SCENE

This party is all about fresh, seasonal produce that inspires both children and their parents. You and your guests can opt to either rendezvous at the market and shop collectively or hit up the markets individually. Either way, you'll be shopping in advance of the gathering, so that you can select your produce and have plenty of time to prepare your dish.

A GARDEN OF COLOR: When considering the color palette for this gathering, I looked to the garden, quite literally. Covering the entire color spectrum, the garden is rife with décor inspiration.

SEASONAL PRODUCE CENTERPIECES: Ask guests to bring some colorful items found while shopping at the farmers' market to put in vases and to arrange decoratively on the table. Leafy greens and beets, carrots, and fennel with their tops on look lovely in tall glass vases, while seasonal peppers, sweet potatoes, and winter squashes are ideal for tablescapes. You can provide vases if you have them, or request that guests bring a vase with them.

MARKET BASKETS: Baskets used for market shopping are often as functional as they are attractive. Ask your guests to bring along a basket if they have one and use them as decorating props around the bottom of the feasting table.

MARKET STORIES

Research has shown that the more engaged and active children are in the growing and preparation of foods, the more willing they are to eat them. Shopping at farmers' markets or gathering items from their own backyard plots, then, is a great opportunity for kids to get excited about food and explore a wide variety of fruits, vegetables, and flavors. Once everyone arrives, have the parents and children gather around the feasting table. Ask the kids to share what they were inspired by at the farmers' market or from their own gardens. Allow them to relay what happened at the market, and then later, at home, as they prepared their dish.

DECORATE MARKET BAGS

Encourage children to get excited about market day by providing them with their own reusable produce bag. Easily sourced online (I found the bags used for this gathering on Etsy) or at natural foods stores, reusable cloth bags made from muslin or another natural light-weight fabric can be customized at the gathering.

YOU WILL NEED

- Craft paper or newspaper
- Reusable cotton cloth bags (1 per child)
- Craft paints
- Paintbrushes

TO MAKE

Cover a table or low, flat work surface with craft paper or newspaper. Allow the children to decorate their bag however they see fit. You may want to suggest that parents bring paint-friendly clothing options or art aprons, as these paints won't be washable.

TIPS FOR MAKING THE MOST OF YOUR MARKET EXPERIENCE

- **Make a loop around the entire market before making any purchases.** This way you'll see what everyone has to offer, what sort of pricing the selections are listed at, and in what quantities.
- **Arrive early for best selection; come late for the best deals.** If you know you've just got to have Farmer Jill's rhubarb, and that her stall is a popular one, or are planning on serving Baker Dave's croissants for brunch, make haste to the market. The early bird gets the best pickings. If it's deals you're after, come late, when farmers might be more inclined to slash prices in order to sell off their wares.
- **Carry smaller bills.** Too many customers presenting $20 bills will quickly dwindle the petty cash vendors have on hand. They'll appreciate smaller bills mightily, and your transaction can be processed much more expediently as well.
- **Use a basket instead of a bag.** While canvas bags have their place (I should know—I own about twenty!), I've found a basket works better at the market. Heavier items like loaves of bread can ride alongside softer items like berries without crushing them.
- **Ask farmers for recipe ideas.** If that celeriac bulb intrigues you, but you haven't the faintest idea how to prepare it, ask your farmer. They'll likely have all sorts of preparation methods to share.
- **Inquire if farms are open for seasonal tours/visits.** Many farms open their property to visitors at some point during the year. A trip to pick apples or harvest dew-kissed strawberries, not to mention simply check out the lay of the land and agricultural methods employed, is a delight on multiple levels.
- **Bring a cooler.** Most farmers' markets occur during warmer months. It would be a shame to have to pass up hand-churned pints of ice cream, dairy-fresh butter,

local artisanal cheeses, or pastured beef simply because of their perishable nature. Pack the cooler with ice or, better yet, reusable ice packs and you, and your purchases, can keep cool.

- **Buy in bulk.** Even if you're not into canning, scoop up a surplus of produce when it's in season and dehydrate or freeze it for later use.
- **Remember meat and dairy.** Farmers' markets often offer the best opportunities to buy local meat and dairy products. Not only can you ask the farmer specific questions about their agricultural and processing methods, you'll often acquire their goods at lower prices.
- **Bring a coffee mug.** Most markets offer a vendor peddling a fine cup of joe. Toting your own mug to market allows you to down hot java while passing on the disposable cups.

Early autumn is an amazing time to work with fresh fruits and vegetables. The late summer crops are in, while the change in weather means cool-loving items are thriving too. Eggplant, figs, arugula, peas, peppers, apples, pears, winter squash, kale, collards, chard, sweet potatoes—there's just so much good stuff to work with now! Children can visit the market or garden and make their selection for the gathering based on their favorite color, favorite shape, or favorite flavor, or, for the more intrepid tiny gourmand, change course entirely and opt for something they've never before tasted. The three recipes offered here all incorporate classic culinary techniques so that children will learn as they cook and bake, such as how to separate egg whites from yolks, whip whites into meringue, create vegetable stock, roast vegetables, chop apples, and puree soup.

MENU SUGGESTIONS

Butternut Squash and Cider Herbed Soup*, Chard, Pasta, and Mozzarella Bake*,

Spiced Apple Pound Cake*, Kale and Cranberry Salad, Cinderella Pumpkin Pie,

Gazpacho, Eggplant and Mozzarella Roll-Ups, Sweet Potato Pie, Sweet Pepper Strata,

Stuffed Acorn Squashes, Cheese Plate with Fig and Thyme Jam, Celeraic Slaw,

Pumpkin and Walnut Bread

BUTTERNUT SQUASH AND CIDER HERBED SOUP

Sweet soups are always popular with the young set. This one gets its kicks from both the squash and some apple cider, another seasonal favorite. The recipe begins with making a vegetable stock, a crucial step in the soup achieving its intense depths of flavor.

Serves 6 to 8

YOU WILL NEED

2 butternut squashes,
   weighing about 5 pounds
   total

5 tablespoons olive oil

1 medium onion, chopped

1 large or 2 small carrots,
   chopped

1 stalk celery, chopped

2 cloves garlic, peeled and
   smashed

3 quarts water

2 teaspoons sea salt

1 cup apple cider

1 cup heavy cream

1 teaspoon fresh thyme

1 teaspoon fresh marjoram

Several grinds of black
   pepper

PREPARE THE SQUASH: Preheat the oven to 400°F.

Cut the tips off of both ends of the butternut squashes, so that they can rest flat when placed upright on a cutting board. Carefully cut the squashes in half lengthwise. Scoop out the seeds. Coat the squashes and a medium baking pan with 2 tablespoons of the olive oil. Roast the squash for 1 hour.

PREPARE THE STOCK: Warm the remaining 3 tablespoons olive oil in a stockpot over medium heat. Add the onion, carrots, and celery and cook for about 6 minutes, until fragrant and the onions become limp. Add the garlic and cook for 2 more minutes. Add the water and salt and stir to combine. Bring to a boil, then reduce the heat to low and simmer for 40 minutes. Strain the stock though a colander into a bowl and return the liquid to the stockpot. Compost, discard, or store the cooked vegetables for later use.

PREPARE THE SOUP: When the squashes are done roasting, remove the baking pan from the oven. Allow to cool, then scoop the cooked flesh out of the peel. Puree the cooked squash in a food processor or mash by hand.

Add the cider, heavy cream, thyme, marjoram, and squash puree to the stockpot containing the stock. Stir well and heat over low heat for 20 minutes, stirring occasionally. Season with pepper. Reheat at the gathering if necessary, and serve warm.

CHARD, PASTA, AND MOZZARELLA BAKE

++++++++++++++++++++++++++++

YOU WILL NEED

5 tablespoons olive oil

1 medium onion, diced

2 carrots, diced

3 cloves garlic, minced

2 bunches Swiss chard,
   cleaned and chopped, with
   the bottom stems cut off

One 28-ounce can
   diced tomatoes

1 cup grated Parmesan
   cheese

1 teaspoon fresh thyme

1 teaspoon fresh marjoram

1 teaspoon sea salt

Several grinds of black
   pepper

1 pound pasta, such as
   rigatoni or elbow macaroni

5 large eggs, beaten

1 pound fresh mozzarella
   cheese, shredded

++++++++++++++++++++++++++++

Noodles and cheese typically receive high marks from children. What they might not typically gravitate toward on their own, however, are leafy greens like chard. Here we've tucked it into a hearty tomato sauce and then partnered it up with the trusty pasta and cheese duo.

Serves 6 to 8

TO MAKE

PREPARE THE SAUCE: In a large saucepan, heat 3 tablespoons of the olive oil over medium heat. Add the onion and carrots and cook for about 6 minutes, until fragrant. Add the garlic and cook for 1 minute. Add the Swiss chard and cook for 5 minutes, stirring frequently. Add the diced tomatoes and cook for 5 minutes. Add the Parmesan cheese, thyme, marjoram, salt, and pepper; stir to combine. Reduce the heat to low and simmer for 30 minutes, stirring occasionally.

PREPARE THE PASTA: Boil a large pot of water and cook the pasta until al dente according to the package's directions. Drain the pasta, then add it to the cooked sauce. Stir well so that the noodles are fully covered in the sauce. Cook for 2 additional minutes, stirring frequently, then turn off the heat.

PREPARE THE DISH: Preheat the oven to 350°F.

Add the beaten eggs to the pasta mixture and stir well. Grease a baking pan with the remaining 2 tablespoons olive oil, then add the pasta mixture to the dish. Bake for 30 minutes.

Remove the dish from the oven and top the noodles with the shredded mozzarella cheese. Bake for 20 more minutes, then remove from the oven. The pasta bake can be served warm or at room temperature.

SPICED APPLE POUND CAKE

Pound cake is a perennial crowd pleaser for young and old alike. Add some seasonal apples and spices and you've got a clear winner. This would also make a great component to a trifle, layered with caramelized apples, fresh whipped cream, and creamy vanilla pudding.

Makes one 9 x 5-inch loaf.

TO MAKE

Preheat the oven to 350°F. Lightly butter a 9 x 5-inch loaf pan. Set aside.

Combine the flour and spices in a medium bowl. Set aside. Beat the egg whites with an electric mixer until light and billowy. Set aside.

In a separate bowl, cream the butter and sugar until light and fluffy, 3 to 4 minutes. Add the egg yolks, one at a time, to the butter and sugar mixture. Scrape the bowl and beaters with a spatula after each addition. Add the vanilla. Using a spatula, gently fold in the beaten egg whites until fully incorporated.

Add the flour and spices to the mixture, in 2 increments, scraping down the bowl and beaters after each addition. Stir in the chopped apples until fully combined with the batter.

YOU WILL NEED

2½ cups all-purpose flour

1 teaspoon ground cinnamon

½ teaspoon ground nutmeg

¼ teaspoon ground cloves

¼ teaspoon ground allspice

4 large eggs, separated

1 cup (2 sticks) unsalted butter, at room temperature

1½ cups sugar

1 teaspoon vanilla extract

2 apples, peeled, cored, and roughly chopped

Pour the batter into the prepared pan. Use a spatula to spread the batter evenly across the pan. Bake for 1½ hours, or until the top is golden brown and a knife inserted into the center comes out clean. Cool in the pan for 15 minutes. Remove from the pan and leave to cool on a wire rack for an additional 15 minutes.

Cut the pound cake down the center using a serrated knife. Then cut the loaf into ½-inch slices.

Apples to Apples

I've yet to meet anyone who didn't like apples. This party celebrates the iconic autumnal fruit that pleases so many, in every permutation imaginable.

MY LIFELONG LOVE AFFAIR with apples is steeped in tradition. The crisp, fragrant fruit has popped up in family meals, festivities, and occasions for as long as I can remember. As a child, apple butter was a much-loved autumnal treat, spread thickly over buttery biscuits. Whenever I make a batch of it now (which I do every year, both traditionally spiced and in a more exotic incarnation, with cardamom, my most beloved spice), fond memories of mornings with my maternal grandmother, Nanny, a long-time apple butter fan, wash over me. A gathering focused on apples, then, is clearly a personal one for me. It's likely one for your guests, too, as it seems a fondness for the fruit has found its way into so many people's lives.

Many weekends in my childhood, apples would make a cameo at the family breakfast table. They'd appear in the form of what we then referred to as "fried apples." Truer more to the spirit than to the letter of frying, Mom would melt a generous portion of either bacon grease or butter in her well-worn cast-iron skillet, add chopped apples, sugar, cinnamon, and a bit of water to the pan, and simmer the mixture into spicy, soft submission. We'd pair the fried apples with homemade biscuits, scrambled eggs, and bacon or sausage and groan in hearty satisfaction.

Bobbing for apples was another way the fruits found their way into my youth. My mom loves celebrations and made a point of throwing truly memorable childhood birthday parties for my brother and me. She'd slice small openings into the sides of firm apples, tuck quarters into them, and send us and our ragtag crew of friends bobbing our way through a bucket of apples and water.

In the late 1990s, my mother relocated to a rural, postage-size, three-stoplight town in western North Carolina. Along with stunning mountain views, her newly acquired 1800s-era farmhouse also included a prolific apple tree. With almost no effort on her part, the tree has repeatedly produced a bountiful harvest each autumn. Deer, passers-by, and I all pilfer the tree (with permission, of course, the deer notwithstanding) for its outstanding specimens. Dark-skinned and perfectly round, her apples are some of the finest I've ever had the pleasure of tasting.

Many are unaware that North America was once host to more than 16,000 varieties of apples. At a lecture I attended given by the conservationist, lecturer, author, and food and farming advocate Gary Nabhan, it was revealed that roughly nine out of ten apple varieties once grown on this land are at risk of permanent extinction. These are apple specimens that have grown and thrived here for centuries, apples perfectly suited to this soil, this climate, and this topography.

The significance of the disappearance of heirloom apples, a fruit so dear to my family and me, left an indelible mark on me during Nabhan's lecture. It has motivated and compelled me to maintain a close relationship with this generationally beloved fruit. My mother's apple tree, the apple orchard I visit every autumn in neighboring Henderson County (the nation's seventh largest apple-producing region), my own apple trees, and all of the future apple trees I intend to plant, nurture, harvest, and eat from will keep the fruit a focal point of my own growing family's history. I plan to never stop engaging in a bit of buttering, frying, bobbing, and much, much more.

Clearly, my friends feel the same way. At this gathering, which I held at a nearby apple orchard, it was evident the fruit represented more than mere sustenance to them as well. Their children ran through the orchards, played on the swing sets, and crunched and munched apple-centric dishes with obvious delight. We all happily and heartily swilled fresh cider, savored the gentle autumn breezes, and sat languidly and contentedly on the orchard's picnic tables, in no particular hurry to be anywhere else. Here's hoping the apple, its legacy, and its future will leave you and your guests satisfied right down to the core.

SETTING THE SCENE

When planning this gathering, I kept returning to images from the film *The Cider House Rules*. Rustic simplicity was what characterized that film and was what inspired and informed my décor decisions here.

APPLE POMANDERS: Decorating with pomanders is a simple way of infusing your gathering with fragrance. And they couldn't be easier to make. Make them yourself or ask guests to bring apples with them, one for each person in their party, as well as one jar of whole cloves per apple they'll be using to make a pomander upon their arrival. Have each guest stud the entire apple with the cloves. If the whole fruit is covered with the spices, placed closely together, it'll last longer. If guests have neither the inclination nor the patience (mine took twenty-three minutes, start to finish), however, to prick the entire fruit, they can also simply make a design, or their initials, or an image in the apple. Once the fruits are decorated, place them around the feasting table to be enjoyed during the event. Guests can then retrieve their pomanders and bring them home once the festivities end. They'll be greatly appreciated by your guests long after the event concludes, imbuing their homes with a heady scent during the autumn and winter months, when the aroma of cloves is where it's at.

AUTUMNAL PICNIC: If you have the lovely fortune of having an apple orchard near your home, hosting this gathering there as an autumnal picnic would be so much fun. Otherwise, find out who has the fire pit or fireplace in your group of loved ones and gather around it to feast!

WOODN'T IT BE NICE? I tried to incorporate wood into this gathering wherever possible. Whether wooden picnic tables, serving utensils, platters, or bowls, wood seems the ideal material for an apple-focused party. After all, apples do grow on trees! Feel free to request that guests bring their dish in a wooden serving vessel if they happen to have one.

SHARING THE EXPERIENCE

APPLE GAMES

Consider playing some apple-themed games at your gathering. Bobbing for apples is perennially popular with the younger set. For the sake of hygiene, provide only one apple in a bucket of water per player. Adults and older kids might enjoy "Johnny Applestack," inspired by a game of the same name I saw on a popular television game show. The goal is to stack five apples one on top of the other, and keep them standing upright for thirty seconds. Last, "Apple Pass," wherein two teams compete by passing an apple under their chin, always elicits loads of laughs. If the apple is dropped, the team must start at the beginning. The first team to pass the apple successfully to each team member wins.

MAKE MULLING SPICE SACHETS

Warm mulled apple cider is one of the most iconic flavors of the season. Skip the store-bought offerings and whip up sachets with your guests. The host may supply all of the components necessary to create the sachets, or each attendee could be asked to supply one ingredient.

Makes 10 sachets (each will infuse 1 gallon of apple cider)

YOU WILL NEED

10 small cinnamon sticks

3 tablespoons green cardamom pods

¼ cup dried orange peel

¼ cup dried lemon peel

3 tablespoons whole cloves

3 tablespoons whole allspice

3 tablespoons black peppercorns

10 star anise

10 small muslin sachets (see
   Note)

TO MAKE

Break the cinnamon sticks in half and place in a medium bowl. Using the back of a spoon, bruise the cardamom pods to reveal their seeds. Add them to the bowl with the cinnamon sticks. Add the remaining ingredients to the bowl. Stir to fully combine.

Place 2 tablespoons of the mixture into each muslin bag. Cinch the top of the bag together, securing the contents inside. When ready to use, bring 1 gallon of apple cider to a boil in a large pot. Add the spice sachet, reduce the heat to low, and simmer for 1 hour. Remove the sachet before serving.

Note: These can be found online or often in natural foods stores' bulk spices and herbs sections. If you will have more than 10 guests at your gathering, simply increase the ingredient quantities accordingly.

Sweet or savory, apples are ideal specimens for cooking with. Chopped, sliced, pureed, what have you, apples are as versatile as they are delicious. So as to avoid everyone showing up with apple pies, ask guests to reply in advance with what dish they'll be making. A two-thirds savory to one-third sweet ratio would be the ideal balance.

MENU SUGGESTIONS

Apple Bourbon Pan Meatloaf*, Rosemary and Sage Apple Hand Pies*,

Apple and Fennel Slaw with Buttermilk Dressing*, Apple Sage Mac and Cheese,

Candied Apples, Apple and Chard Quiche, Cabbage and Apple Stir-fry,

Apple, Onion, and Cheddar Frittata, Apple Butter Brie en Croute, Caramel Apple Pie,

Turkey and Apple Potpie, Couscous Apple Salad, Sausage and Apple Rolls

APPLE BOURBON PAN MEATLOAF

Many a meatloaf is rendered dry, bland, and tough on account of overcooking, under-seasoning, and inadequate moisture. Here, eggs, milk, and fresh apples provide ample moisture, while fresh herbs and a sweet and savory glaze take this loaf to the meatloaf hall of fame. The loaf is spread out in a baking pan rather than the more common bread pan. I've discovered that doing so helps the loaf cook more uniformly.

Serves 4 to 6

YOU WILL NEED

- 1 tablespoon unsalted butter
- 2 ounces bourbon
- 2 to 3 medium apples, peeled, cored, and cubed
- 2½ pounds ground grass-fed sirloin
- 3 cups fresh breadcrumbs (or 1 cup dried)
- 4 large eggs
- ⅓ cup milk
- 2 teaspoons sea salt
- 2 tablespoons soy sauce
- 1 tablespoon finely chopped fresh sage (or 1 teaspoon dried)
- 1 tablespoon finely chopped fresh rosemary

- 2 cloves garlic, minced, or 1 teaspoon dried garlic granules
- Several grinds of black pepper
- Olive oil for the baking sheet

FOR THE TOPPING

- ½ cup ketchup
- ½ cup apple butter
- Splash of bourbon
- ½ teaspoon garlic granules
- Pinch of sea salt
- Several grinds of black pepper
- A few drops of hot sauce (optional)

TO MAKE

PREPARE THE FILLING: Preheat the oven to 375°F. Lightly grease a baking sheet (the size of the baking sheet isn't important; we used a 9 × 12-inch sheet pan, but what

matters is that the loaf be about 1½ inches thick). I used olive oil, but a neutral-flavored oil such as canola works equally well.

Melt the butter with the bourbon in a sauté pan over medium heat. Add the apples and sauté for about 10 minutes, until they start to break down. Remove from the heat and transfer to a large bowl. Add the meat and stir to fully combine. Add the breadcrumbs to the meat and apple mixture.

In a separate bowl, whisk the eggs, milk, and salt together. Add to the meat mixture and stir to combine. Add the soy sauce, sage, rosemary, garlic, and pepper. Mix well (clean hands are best for this task!).

ASSEMBLE THE LOAF: Form a flat loaf on the greased baking sheet, about 1½ inches thick. Mix all of the ingredients for the topping in a small bowl. Smooth the mixture evenly across the top of the loaf.

Cook for 1 hour (we put some sweet potatoes into the oven at the same time to bake while the meatloaf cooked). Place under the broiler for 2 to 4 minutes, until the crust starts to brown a little. Allow the loaf to rest for a few minutes before serving.

ROSEMARY AND SAGE APPLE HAND PIES

These lovely little treats make pie eating imminently transportable. The aromatic, resinous flavors of sage and rosemary are a perfect foil to the fruit's sweetness.

Makes 12 to 14 hand pies

YOU WILL NEED

FOR THE CINNAMON SUGAR

2 tablespoons granulated sugar

1 teaspoon ground cinnamon

Basic Pie Dough (page 17)

FOR THE FILLING

1 pound apples (such as Gala, Granny Smith, Jonagold, or a blend of baking apples), peeled, cored, and finely chopped

2 tablespoons lemon juice

Zest of 1 lemon

3 tablespoons light brown sugar

2 tablespoons minced fresh sage

1 tablespoon minced fresh rosemary

1 tablespoon all-purpose flour

½ teaspoon ground cinnamon

FOR THE EGG WASH

1 egg yolk

1 tablespoon cold water

TO MAKE

PREPARE THE CINNAMON SUGAR: Combine the sugar and cinnamon in a small bowl. Stir to fully blend. Set aside.

PREPARE THE HAND PIE CIRCLES: Remove 1 of the chilled pie dough disks from the refrigerator. Roll it out into a 12- to 14-inch circle on a lightly floured surface. Cut out six to seven 5-inch rounds, rerolling scraps as necessary. Transfer the dough rounds onto a baking parchment– or silicone mat–lined cookie sheet.

Repeat the above steps with the second chilled dough disk. Refrigerate both cookie sheets while preparing the filling.

PREPARE THE FILLING: Place all of the filling ingredients together in a large bowl. Stir to fully combine.

ASSEMBLE THE HAND PIES: Preheat the oven to 375°F.

Remove the sheets of chilled dough rounds from the refrigerator. Mound 1 to 2 tablespoons of the apple mixture on one half of each dough round. Depending on how many dough rounds you cut out, you may have a bit of filling left over.

Fold the other half of the dough round up and over the apple mixture. Crimp and seal the edges together using the tines of a fork. Using a pointy-tip knife, cut a small X over the center of each hand pie. This enables steam to vent off while the pies are baking.

Beat the egg yolk with the cold water. Brush lightly over the top of each hand pie. Sprinkle each of the pies with a pinch of cinnamon sugar. Bake for 30 minutes, or until the crusts are golden brown, rotating the positions of the cookie sheets midway through the baking time.

APPLE AND FENNEL SLAW WITH BUTTERMILK DRESSING

An autumn slaw is a great recipe to have in your culinary repertoire. Though it often makes appearances at summer gatherings, coleslaw is wonderful made with the produce of this season too. I used a red cabbage here for color contrast, but green works equally well. Any apple variety will do, but be sure that, whatever you choose, it's quite ripe and crisp.

Serves 6 to 8

TO MAKE

Using a food processor, mandoline, or sharp knife, shred the cabbage into fine pieces. Transfer to a large bowl. Shred the fennel bulbs, but not as fine as the cabbage. Add to the bowl with the cabbage. Core the apples and cut them into small julienned strips. Toss the apple strips in the lemon juice as you go to keep the apples from browning. Add to the cabbage and fennel.

Mix together the remaining ingredients (except for the fennel fronds) in a large bowl until fully combined. Pour the dressing over the cabbage, fennel, and apples, and stir in about three-quarters of the fennel fronds. Stir together until everything is well coated with dressing.

When ready to serve, transfer the mixture to a serving bowl. Sprinkle the remaining few fennel fronds decoratively across the top as a garnish.

YOU WILL NEED

1 small head red cabbage

2 fennel bulbs (reserve and chop the feathery fronds)

4 apples

2 tablespoons lemon juice

1 cup buttermilk

½ cup mayonnaise

½ cup apple cider vinegar

3 tablespoons sugar

1 tablespoon prepared mustard

1 tablespoon sea salt

2 teaspoons ground coriander

2 teaspoons celery seeds

A few grinds of black pepper

The Great Pumpkin

No mention of autumn is complete without a nod to pumpkins. This gathering honors the seasonal orbs and all of the craft, décor, and gustatory delights they offer.

I'VE NEVER BEEN much of one for superlatives. Labeling things the "best" or "worst" or my "favorite" has never come naturally to me. That said, if I were forced to choose my preferred season, it would definitely be autumn. And directly in tandem with my adoration for gorgeous foliage, warm sweaters, and hot mugs of apple cider would be a profound and abiding love of all things pumpkin. They're lovely to look at, delectable to consume, and immensely fun to decorate, carve, and otherwise festoon for festive occasions. A gathering centered on pumpkins is an opportunity to enjoy an ephemeral, annual food and all of the goodness that it brings.

My recollections of pumpkin-centric joys are myriad. There is the enjoyment of the glorious, rotund crop itself, a food loved by my entire extended family. Pumpkin pies were the source of much "oohing" and "ahhing" every Thanksgiving. My older brother, a November baby, adores pumpkin pie and would have it for every meal, given his druthers. There is also pumpkin ice cream, a treat said brother and I would clamor for each autumn from a local dairy farm. We'd order up a hearty scoop flecked with cinnamon, cloves, nutmeg, and allspice and eat our cones with immeasurable happiness.

More recently, I discovered a new pumpkin incarnation that will without question work its way into my culinary repertoire. The dish I encountered was served at Franny's, a restaurant in Brooklyn, New York, with a heavy emphasis on local foods. There, pumpkin was first roasted, then pureed, and finally adorned with pieces of chopped apples, celery, and walnuts and drizzled with olive oil. It was utterly simple in its execution and completely sublime in its flavor. Another humble, yet flawless, example of just how much pumpkin can shine with little in the way of embellishment.

Then, of course, there's the pumpkin lore of my childhood. When I was about seven or eight years old, I was an overnight guest at a sleepaway camp. Although it was summer, the camp counselors decided to build a large bonfire and tell ghost stories. This particular camp was located on Sleepy Hollow Road in northern Virginia, so, naturally, *The Legend of Sleepy Hollow* with its headless horseman, Ichabod Crane, had to be told. As the counselor telling the tale concluded the story, another one suddenly exclaimed, "Look! What's that thing in the distance? Is that a horse?!" It turned out the staff had decided to play a joke on us poor young children and spook us into believing a horse had broken out of the camp's stables on a nocturnal quest to find its pumpkin-headed rider. Suffice to say, we were terrified. Although my passion for pumpkins has endured over the years, ever since that youthful fright I've never quite looked at pumpkins and their terror-inducing potential in the same way.

It's amazing how a food can serve as the unofficial declaration that a season is in full swing. That was certainly the case when I hosted this gathering. As I gathered with friends and family on my patio one glorious afternoon in late October to carve pumpkins and enjoy a buffet of pumpkin eats, it was almost like an inaudible announcement reverberated through the crowd. "It's here! It's here! Autumn is truly here, friends!" it seemed to say. The changing foliage all around us, the spicy and sweet aromas of the dishes guests had brought, the flaming hues of the pumpkins we crafted and decorated with, and the bonfire we warmed ourselves by gave us definitive confirmation that fall was very much happening.

During this gathering, consider all of the joys pumpkins have brought you over the seasons, as they have me. Maybe it was a pumpkin doughnut enjoyed at a country farm's pumpkin patch. Perhaps it was pumpkin-smashing shenanigans engaged in during adrenaline-fueled teenage years. Quite possibly it was an annual family viewing of *It's the Great Pumpkin, Charlie Brown,* featuring Charles Schulz's much-loved Peanuts gang. Whatever your memories reveal, they're bound to be filled with happiness. Here's to carving out more pumpkin-centric joy!

SETTING THE SCENE

This party is a serious delight for all of the senses. From the flavors to the colors, the smooth texture to the fleshy scent, a gathering for pumpkins is silly, savory, sweet, and sensational!

AN INSPIRED PALETTE: While the food is clearly the heavy emphasis here, for me, this party is also all about the vivid colors of the pumpkins themselves. Invoke the wide range of colors pumpkins come in by incorporating green, white, gray-blue, and, of course, orange shades in everything from linens to tableware. I even seized the opportunity to dress like a pumpkin and put on a pair of bright orange pants!

PUMPKIN VASES: Decorating the feasting areas with little pumpkin-filled vases is both gorgeous to behold and easy to pull off, a definite win-win in my book. Ask guests to bring a smaller pumpkin along with the one they'll be carving. Carve off the pumpkins' tops and fill them with tea lights, votive candles, or dried botanical elements foraged on-site or brought with the guests. When guests depart, be sure to send their vases home with them.

A PUMPKIN PATCH: How much fun would it be to have this party in a pumpkin patch? Guests could go directly from the field to the carving table, decorating their selections in a truly inspired setting. Many pick-your-own patches typically have picnic tables where you and your guests could set up after picking out your pumpkins. You might want to call ahead and make sure that outside food is permitted.

PUMPKIN TALES, HALLOWEEN HIJINKS, AND GHOST STORIES

A pumpkin-centric gathering is a perfect opportunity for guests to share all manner of recollections. Since pumpkins are so often associated with Halloween, it would be fun to hear folks talk about a memorable pumpkin patch they visited, or Halloween costume they donned, or even a ghost story they once heard that really got under their skin. Ask what comes to mind when the word *pumpkin* is uttered and let the memories come to life!

CARVE PUMPKINS

YOU WILL NEED

- Carving tools
- Cookie cutters
- Pumpkins

While they're delicious to eat, pumpkins are equally well loved for their appearance, not to mention the myriad ways their looks can be customized. Ask guests to bring one carving pumpkin per family, or more if their family is large or they have children who might want their own pumpkin. If they have any tools that would work for carving, they can bring those as well. You'll need a variety of carving spoons, knives, and other tools for decorating; cookie cutters are handy too (just use a mallet to pound them through the pumpkin's flesh). Have guests save the seeds for roasting if they're so inclined. Otherwise, put out a communal bowl for the seeds and filling. If chickens are on hand, they'll be happy to take care of the pumpkin leftovers!

TO MAKE

Place newspaper or craft paper over a large table. Pile carving tools in the center. After guests arrive and get settled in, encourage them to decorate their pumpkin in whatever way they see fit!

COOKING IT UP

When it comes to pumpkin dishes, think beyond pumpkin pie. While that scrumptious dessert is a perennial pleaser come holiday season, pumpkin is an incredibly malleable food, making it ideal for both sweet and savory dishes alike. From soul-satisfying, robust lasagnas to creamy, warm soups, from spicy seed brittle to smooth pumpkin butter paired with fresh figs and pumpernickel, pumpkin is a food lover's best friend!

MENU SUGGESTIONS

Pumpkin and Sage Lasagna*, Pumpkin and Cranberry Chutney*,

Bombay Pumpkin Cupcakes with Cardamom Cream Cheese Frosting*,

Spiced Pulled Pork with Pumpkin Barbecue Sauce, Pumpkin Soup with Bacon,

Pumpkin Molé Tacos, Apple and Pumpkin Seed Waldorf Salad,

Pumpkin Stuffing, Pumpkin Ale, Roasted Pumpkin with Rigatoni and Swiss Chard,

Pumpkin Puree with Chopped Celery and Walnuts, Pumpkin Bars,

Pumpkin Bread Pudding with Spiced Rum Whipped Topping

PUMPKIN AND SAGE LASAGNA

Using a bounty of seasonal offerings, this lasagna wins on both the visual and flavor fronts. Pumpkin, kale, and sage are combined with breakfast sausage, tomatoes, ricotta, and a hint of nutmeg for a dish that's substantive, delicious, and well received, if the pan I prepared that was gobbled up in minutes is any indication!

Serves 8 to 10

YOU WILL NEED

FOR THE MEAT SAUCE

¼ cup olive oil

1 medium onion, diced

3 to 4 cloves garlic, minced

1½ pounds breakfast sausage meat

Leaves of 1 bunch kale,
    rinsed and chopped

One 28-ounce can diced tomatoes

½ cup red or white wine

1 teaspoon sea salt

½ teaspoon freshly grated nutmeg

Several grinds of black pepper

2 tablespoons all-purpose flour

FOR THE LASAGNA

One 16-ounce package lasagna noodles

Butter for greasing the baking pan

3 cups shredded mozzarella cheese

FOR THE RICOTTA PUMPKIN FILLING

¼ cup sage leaves, finely minced

2 tablespoons olive oil

Two 15-ounce containers ricotta cheese

2 cups pumpkin puree

1 large egg, beaten

½ teaspoon sea salt

½ teaspoon freshly grated nutmeg

TO MAKE

PREPARE THE MEAT SAUCE: Heat the olive oil in a large sauté pan over medium heat. Add the onion and sauté for about 10 minutes, until it becomes fragrant and turns a little brown at the edges. Add the garlic and cook, stirring, for 1 to 2 minutes. Add the sausage and cook, stirring every minute or so, until browned, about 5 minutes. Add the kale and cook down, stirring occasionally, for 10 minutes. Add the tomatoes, wine, salt, nutmeg, and pepper. Reduce the heat to medium-low and simmer for 25 to 30 minutes. Add the flour and stir to completely incorporate.

Cook the meat sauce for another 5 minutes, then remove from the heat. Prepare the lasagna noodles according to the package's instructions. While the noodles boil, make the ricotta filling.

PREPARE THE RICOTTA FILLING: Place the minced sage leaves and olive oil in a food processor and pulse briefly to combine. If you don't have a food processor, you can simply blend the sage and oil together in a small bowl using a fork. Combine the sage pesto with the remaining ricotta filling ingredients in a medium bowl. Set aside.

ASSEMBLE THE LASAGNA: Preheat the oven to 350°F.

Liberally grease a 9 x 13-inch baking pan with butter. Spread roughly one-third of the meat sauce over the bottom of the baking pan. Sprinkle ½ cup of the shredded mozzarella across the sauce.

Place 4 lasagna noodles over the mozzarella, overlapping their edges as needed. Spread roughly one-third of the ricotta filling across the noodles. Sprinkle ½ cup of shredded mozzarella across the ricotta. Place 4 lasagna noodles over the mozzarella.

Repeat the above steps twice more, with layers of the remaining meat sauce and ricotta filling, divided by lasagna noodles and scattered with cheese, ending with a layer of noodles on top. Scatter the remaining 1 cup of mozzarella evenly across the surface of the noodles. Bake for 45 minutes, or until the cheese is evenly browned across the surface of the dish.

Cool for 30 to 45 minutes before serving. The lasagna can be made 1 to 2 days ahead. To serve, reheat at 200°F for about 30 minutes, until the dish is warm to the touch.

PUMPKIN AND CRANBERRY CHUTNEY

Chutney and the cool, crisp weather of autumn are a natural pairing in my book. I love the complexity of flavors presented in its sour and sweet profile. Here I've added other seasonal foods, including apples and cranberries. Pair this chunky chutney with goat cheese or Brie, or a strong cheese such as Gruyère, perhaps some fresh figs or pear slices, and a bit of dark wheat or pumpernickel bread for a well-rounded homage to autumn. Should you come across a seasonal pumpkin ale, I highly recommend adding some to the feast!

Makes 4 to 5 cups

TO MAKE

Combine all of the ingredients in a heavy-bottom large saucepan or Dutch oven. Stir gently to fully combine. Bring the mixture to a gentle boil over medium heat. Reduce the heat to low and simmer uncovered for 1 hour, stirring occasionally to prevent the chutney from sticking to the bottom of the pan.

Remove from the heat, cover with a lid, cool slightly, and then transfer to a serving bowl. The chutney can be made up to 3 days beforehand and kept refrigerated. Warm slightly or allow to come to room temperature before serving.

YOU WILL NEED

- 2 pounds baking pumpkin, peeled, seeded, and roughly chopped
- 1 apple, peeled, cored, quartered, and roughly chopped
- 1 onion, chopped
- ½ cup dried or ¼ cup fresh cranberries
- ½ cup dried currants
- ⅔ cup granulated sugar
- ⅓ cup dark brown sugar
- 1½ cups apple cider vinegar
- 1 cup water
- 2 teaspoon brown mustard seeds
- 1 teaspoon ground cinnamon
- 1 teaspoon ground ginger
- ½ teaspoon ground cloves
- ½ teaspoon ground allspice
- Pinch of sea salt

BOMBAY PUMPKIN CUPCAKES WITH CARDAMOM CREAM CHEESE FROSTING

These cupcakes are my tribute to the sweets of India that I love so very much. Cardamom, ginger, cinnamon, and black pepper are combined with pumpkin in the cupcakes, while a generous dose of cardamom is added to the cream cheese frosting. When I served these at the gathering, a guest stopped me in midconversation to declare them the "best cupcakes I've ever eaten." Folks, I believe we have a winner!

Makes 2 dozen cupcakes

YOU WILL NEED

FOR THE CUPCAKES

- 3 cups all-purpose flour
- 1½ teaspoons baking powder
- 1½ teaspoons baking soda
- 2 teaspoons ground cardamom
- 1 teaspoon ground ginger
- 1 teaspoon ground cinnamon
- 1 teaspoon ground black pepper
- ½ teaspoon sea salt
- 1 cup (2 sticks) unsalted butter, melted and slightly cooled
- 1 cup granulated sugar
- ¾ cup light brown sugar
- 1¾ cups pumpkin puree, at room temperature
- 4 large eggs

FOR THE FROSTING

- 3 cups powdered sugar
- ½ cup unsalted butter, at room temperature
- 8 ounces cream cheese, at room temperature
- 2 teaspoons ground cardamom
- 1 teaspoon vanilla extract

TO MAKE

Preheat the oven to 350°F.

Line muffin tins with paper cupcake liners. In a medium bowl, sift together the flour, baking powder, baking soda, spices, and salt. Set aside.

Using an electric mixer on low-medium speed, beat the melted butter, sugars, and pumpkin puree together until light and fluffy. Beat in the eggs one at a time, scraping down the bowl with a spatula after each addition. With the mixer on low speed, gradually beat in the flour mixture until everything is fully blended.

Fill each paper liner with about ¼ cup of batter. Bake for 22 to 25 minutes, until the tops are firm and a knife inserted into the center of a cupcake comes out clean. Cool completely on a wire rack before frosting.

Using an electric mixer, beat all of the frosting ingredients together at medium-high speed until smooth. Frost the cooled cupcakes. Serve immediately, or store in a lidded container for up to 1 day and serve at room temperature.

In Touch with Your Roots

When the weather turns cooler, it's time to put down roots. This gathering honors all things root vegetable in tandem with engendering community roots.

WHEN COLDER WEATHER MOVES IN, woodstoves and fireplaces begin to be tended to, hot soups become the most wonderful thing imaginable, and wool socks work to take the chill off. Simultaneous with these mercury-dipping activities, root vegetables make their welcome move onto the culinary scene. Defined as the underground part of plants used as vegetables, root vegetables grow and thrive while their heat-loving compatriots wither and die. A gathering based around root vegetables provides an opportunity to feast on these delicious seasonal crops and to consider and reflect on the larger idea of putting down roots in one's community.

In my other books, I've discussed a range of small-scale homesteading topics, including how to raise chickens, keep bees, create homemade dairy products, and preserve the harvest through home canning. During my research on these topics, both online and in person, I made a pivotal discovery. While some of these skills were ones I'd possessed for some time, others were wholly uncharted territory for me. I found I needed mentors, both on my computer and in the real, tactile world of chicken feathers and honeybee smokers.

As I began connecting with area farmers, beekeepers, cheese makers, and long-time canners, I discovered a seasoned, wise, skilled pool of individuals, right in my own neighborhood. These were folks I might not have otherwise encountered, owing to our collective differences in age, gender, political stance, and more. Despite those barriers, though, our mutual interests in homesteading pursuits drew us together and connected us with a singularity of purpose I never anticipated. I held the gathering pictured here at my friend Natalie's urban homesteading supply store, Villagers, located in Asheville, North Carolina. In addition to offering retail items for sale, her shop also holds classes and is a general hub of community activity, making it the perfect setting for such a gathering.

So what's the connection between root vegetables and community? A good deal, it turns out. Root vegetables draw nourishment from deep down within the soil surrounding them, concentrating a variety of minerals, vitamins, and other plant-based nutrients inside their flesh. They grow and thrive in weather that would destroy other plants, persevering in harsh climates. The elements necessary for developing strong communities are similar. By tapping deep into the outlying body of individuals and gathering up the skill sets collectively held, communities grow and flourish.

A gathering celebrating the hardiness of root vegetables and community is ideal for this time of year as well. During colder, less hospitable weather, root vegetables were historically a source of food, quite literally keeping humans and animals alive. Our connections and ties and information sharing with members of our communities can similarly sustain us. Several winters ago, when an unexpected snowstorm blocked our one-mile road with downed trees and took out our power for five days, it was our neighbors who helped us saw the trees. It was also our neighbors who loaned us their battery-powered radio so that we could remain in touch with the goings-on of the world beyond our snowed-in cove.

Root vegetables and community roots alike have nourished my body, my home, and my soul. I made new friends at this party, guests Natalie invited whom she thought I'd enjoy meeting. She couldn't have been more correct. Not only did we share delicious root-centric foods and community events and happenings we thought others should know about, we put down the roots of friendship, and have been cultivating them with love and gratitude ever since. As you and your guests

come together to acknowledge, discover, and honor the connections that unify us in our distinct areas of the globe, my sincere hope is that you are left just as revitalized, invigorated, and inspired as I have been.

SETTING THE SCENE

This gathering is a wonderful opportunity to sample the season's earthy delights while connecting with your community. Informal, informative, and inspirational, a roots party should be as comfortable as possible, to permit the greatest opportunities for establishing lasting relationships.

FEEL THE BEET: Embrace the gorgeous hues offered by beets. From deep crimson to vibrant orange, beets present a broad range of seasonally appropriate colors to model your décor after. Tablecloths, napkins, and even dinnerware can all borrow from the beet at this gathering.

ROOT VEGETABLE CENTERPIECE: For this gathering, I wanted to make sure that the actual root vegetables were given their due day in the sun. To that end, I found slices of basswood in various sizes at a large craft supply store. I used a drill to make small pilot holes in the wood at intermittent distances from one another. Then I hammered several three-inch stainless-steel nails into the pilot holes (be sure to use stainless-steel nails if you have any intention of consuming the root veggies later, as galvanized nails have a coating that renders food unsafe to eat). Ask each guest to bring one or two root vegetables with them. Once they arrive, they can put their vegetables on the nails. It's helpful to drill small holes into the vegetables first, as it makes them easier to place on the nail heads. When the gathering concludes, be sure to send your friends home with their produce.

WRITE IT DOWN: During the shared experience portion of this gathering, everyone will be relaying information about community events. It would be helpful to have somewhere to write it all down. Consider a chalkboard, dry-erase board, or similar writing surface, along with having pens and small pieces of paper on hand.

DRESS THE PART: If you think your guests might be up for it, ask them to come dressed in a root vegetable–colored garment. I wore an earthy-green-hued dress to this gathering, conjuring the leafy greens topping the beloved tubers.

COMMUNITY ROOTS

Ask each guest to come prepared to share some community resource with the group. For instance, I'm part of a local online chat forum related to mothers, parenting, and children in general. It's a tremendous resource that many folks haven't heard of. I like to tell every parent I meet about it, so sharing it with my guests at this gathering is one way I can bring a valuable community connection to the attention of others. Guests can simply mention the name of a community resource or bring cards or similar materials to share.

YOU WILL NEED

- 4 cups water
- 2 tablespoons chopped fresh ginger
- 1 tablespoon chopped dried sarsaparilla root
- 1 tablespoon chopped dried sassafras root
- ½ tablespoon chopped dried licorice root
- ½ tablespoon chopped dried burdock root (or 2 table- spoons fresh)
- ½ tablespoon dried winter- green leaves
- 3 star anise
- 4 cups brown sugar

MAKE ROOT BEER

A roots party wouldn't be complete, I feel, without whipping up a batch of root beer! In this recipe, a simple syrup is made and then added (to taste) to sparkling water. Ask guests to bring a 4- to 6-ounce bottle with them for taking some syrup home in. Keep in mind that the syrup needs 2 hours to steep before it's ready for bottling, so plan its cooking schedule at the gathering accordingly.

Makes 4 cups (enough for eight ½ cup servings)

In a medium saucepan, combine the water, ginger, sarsaparilla, sassafras, licorice, burdock, wintergreen, and star anise. Bring to a gentle simmer and cook uncovered for 15 minutes. Add the brown sugar, stirring until it fully dissolves. Remove the saucepan from the heat, cover with a lid, and cool to room temperature, about 2 hours.

Strain the liquid from the solids through a fine-mesh sieve into a bottle or jar. Label, cover with a lid, and store in the refrigerator. Use within 6 months. To serve, begin by placing 2 to 3 tablespoons of syrup in a 12- to 16-ounce jar. Top the syrup off with sparkling water and ice. Add more syrup if you prefer a sweeter root beer.

COOKING IT UP

From gratins to soufflés, hashes to mashes, the sky's the limit when it comes to root vegetables. They can be pureed into warming soups or roasted into caramelized nuggets. Beets, carrots, turnips, and potatoes might be the first root vegetables to come to mind, but don't overlook celeriac, sunchokes (also known as Jerusalem artichokes), rutabagas, horseradish, burdock, daikon, or parsnips. Aromatics like ginger and turmeric should also be considered.

MENU SUGGESTIONS

Sorghum-Glazed Roasted Root Vegetables*, Mashed Root Vegetable Casserole*,
Chocolate, Orange, and Beet Flourless Cake*, Arugula Salad with Roasted Beets,
Bruschetta with Roasted Sweet Potatoes, Feta Cheese, and Honey, Pickled Daikon,
Spicy Carrot Slaw, Roasted Sunchokes and Kale, Borscht with Crème Fraîche, Burdock Root,
Chips, Ginger Hot Toddies, Sweet Potato Pie, Pear, Cranberry, and Ginger Crisp

SORGHUM-GLAZED ROASTED ROOT VEGETABLES

A sweetener indigenous to the southern United States, sorghum was what everyone reached for until the sugar cane barons pushed it out of common use. It's a type of grass, and its sticky liquid is thick like honey while offering not quite as strong a flavor as molasses. It's the perfect partner for roasted root vegetables, as you'll soon discover here.

Serves 6 to 8

TO MAKE

Preheat the oven to 400°F. Lightly oil a 9 x 13-inch baking pan. Set aside.

Place all of the vegetables, the olive oil, rosemary, salt, and pepper in a large bowl. Using either clean hands or a serving spoon, toss until the oil evenly coats all of the vegetable pieces.

Spread the vegetables evenly in the baking pan. Bake for 45 minutes. Remove the pan from the oven, stir the sorghum evenly into the vegetables, and continue baking for an additional 25 to 30 minutes, until the vegetables have softened and are slightly browned.

Cool for 15 to 20 minutes. When ready to serve, transfer to a serving bowl.

Note: If you're unable to find sorghum, molasses can be substituted; reduce the amount to ⅓ cup.

YOU WILL NEED

1 pound carrots, chopped

1 pound beets, peeled and chopped

1½ pounds rutabaga, peeled and chopped

1½ pounds turnips, peeled and chopped

3 tablespoons olive oil

1 tablespoon minced fresh rosemary

1 teaspoon sea salt

Several grinds of fresh black pepper

½ cup sorghum (see Note)

MASHED ROOT VEGETABLE CASSEROLE

A sort of crustless cottage pie, this casserole has "comfort food" written all over it. Mashed yellow potatoes, celeriac, and parsnips crown a sausage filling laced with allspice and thyme. This is what you want to serve when the leaves have all browned and the woodstove is just getting going for the season.

Serves 8 to 10

YOU WILL NEED

FOR THE MASHED TOPPING

½ teaspoon plus a pinch of sea salt

1½ pounds celeriac, peeled and cubed

1½ pounds yellow potatoes (such as Yukon gold), peeled and cubed

1 pound parsnips, peeled and cubed

4 large eggs, separated

6 tablespoons unsalted butter, melted

1 cup heavy cream

1 teaspoon dried thyme (or ½ teaspoon fresh)

FOR THE MEAT FILLING

1 tablespoon olive oil

½ medium onion, diced

2 to 3 cloves garlic, minced

2 pounds ground sausage

2 teaspoons ground allspice

2 teaspoons dried thyme (or 1 teaspoon fresh)

Several grinds of black pepper

Pinch of sea salt

2 tablespoons all-purpose flour

FOR THE TOPPING

1 cup breadcrumbs

TO MAKE

Lightly oil a 9 x 13-inch baking pan. Set aside.

PREPARE THE MASHED TOPPING: Bring 2 quarts of water and a pinch of salt to

boil in a large saucepan. Add the celeriac, potatoes, and parsnips and simmer for 25 minutes. Drain the vegetables and place them in a large bowl.

In a small bowl, beat the egg yolks. In a separate bowl, whisk the egg whites until frothy (beating the whites and yolks separately will add a bit of lightness to the finished casserole). Using a potato masher or large spoon, mash the cooked vegetables with the butter, cream, egg yolks and whites, the ½ teaspoon salt, and the thyme. Set aside.

PREPARE THE SAUSAGE FILLING: Heat the olive oil in a large saucepan or skillet over medium heat. Add the onion and cook until slightly browned and fragrant, 4 to 5 minutes. Add the garlic and cook until lightly browned, 3 to 4 minutes. Add the sausage and stir to blend it into the onions and garlic. Cook for 5 minutes.

Add the allspice, thyme, pepper, and salt. Continue cooking over medium heat until the meat has browned and is cooked throughout, 5 to 7 minutes longer. Add the flour to the meat mixture, stir to fully combine, and cook for an additional 3 to 4 minutes, until the meat thickens slightly. Remove from the heat and set aside.

ASSEMBLE THE CASSEROLE: Preheat the oven to 375°F.

Spread the meat filling evenly across the bottom of the prepared baking pan. Spread the mashed vegetables evenly over the meat. Bake for 30 to 35 minutes, until the mashed topping just begins to brown.

Spread the breadcrumbs evenly across the top of the casserole. Return the baking pan to the oven and bake for an additional 15 minutes, until the breadcrumbs are golden brown and the dish feels firm in the center.

Cool for at least 15 to 20 minutes or up to 30 minutes before serving.

CHOCOLATE, ORANGE, AND BEET FLOURLESS CAKE

While beets in a cake might not be the first way you'd think to use them, after one bite of this cake they'll certainly not be your last. Moist, decadent, with just the faintest hint of citrus, this cake might just become your favorite way to eat your vegetables!

Serves 6 to 8

YOU WILL NEED

½ pound beets

1 pound semisweet choco- late, chopped

½ cup (1 stick) unsalted butter

6 large eggs, separated

¾ cup sugar

1 teaspoon vanilla extract

¼ teaspoon sea salt

2 teaspoons baking powder

Zest of 1 orange

TO MAKE

Trim the stems and ends from the beets. Cut them into quarters, with the peel on. Place in a pot of boiling water and simmer for 35 to 40 minutes, until the beets can be easily pierced with a fork. Prepare an ice-water bath by adding a generous amount of ice cubes to a large bowl. Fill about three-quarters full with cold water. When the beets are done, plunge

them into the ice bath. Within a few minutes, they'll be cool enough to handle and you can easily slide their peels off. Compost or discard the peels.

Using a food processor, in pulsing intervals process the beets until they are fully confetti-minced. Alternately, you can grate the beets and then mince them finely with a large kitchen knife.

Preheat the oven to 350°F. Butter a 9-inch springform pan. Set aside.

Melt the chocolate and butter in a double boiler (if you don't have a double boiler, you can easily fashion one by placing a metal bowl atop a pot containing 1 to 2 inches of boiling water; the bowl above shouldn't ever come into contact with the water below). Meanwhile, whip the egg whites with a mixer or whisk until soft peaks form, 5 to 7 minutes. In a separate bowl, whisk the egg yolks until fully blended.

Whisk the sugar into the melted chocolate and butter mixture. Remove the top bowl of the double boiler and set it onto the kitchen counter. Whisk in the beaten egg yolks, vanilla, salt, baking powder, orange zest, and beets. Using a spatula, gently fold the beaten egg whites into the chocolate mixture. You don't want to deflate them, so take your time here and incorporate them slowly and steadily.

Spread the batter evenly into the prepared pan. Bake for 40 to 45 minutes, until a knife or toothpick inserted into the center of the cake comes out clean. Cool for at least 1 hour before serving.

WINTER

Winter Wonderland

Icy days, a silver-blue tint to everything, and the soft, still flicker of candles character-ize the shift to winter. This gathering honors all of the delicious and gorgeous tastes and sights of the season.

THE DAYS OF EARLY WINTER are very magical ones, aren't they? So much baking and wrapping and gifting and goodness going on inside, with an equal mea-sure of glorious scenery outdoors. The excitement in the air is downright palpable. As the merriment and attendant business of the season envelop us, it's nice to take an evening to slow down and reflect on the foods and botanical elements annually enjoyed come the month of December. A gathering highlighting those things that nourish our bodies and enrich our senses will become a highly treasured affair, long after the tree has come down, the last cup of eggnog has been sipped, and the final gift has been exchanged.

Years ago, long before I became a parent, I knew that I wanted to regularly host seasonal celebrations. The way that nature morphs from one state to the next, pre-senting sensory treats of every kind in a gradual unfolding, was something I felt should be honored and appreciated. Growing up in a Christian household, I knew the meaning ascribed to celebrations from that perspective. As an adult, though, operating from more of a spiritual vantage point than a religious one, I longed to know more about the elements that characterize holidays and gatherings. I was cu-rious about why the colors red and white were associated with Christmas, why eggs factored so heavily into Easter, and why hearts and flowers were connected to Valentine's Day.

Which is how I came to be so captivated by the traditions surrounding the holiday season. I wanted to be able to explain to my future children why it is that people bring evergreen trees into their homes, and why poinsettias adorn tables and mantels, and what Yule logs represent, and why cinnamon and cloves and nutmeg are in such heavy rotation this time of year. Knowing not just that these items appear come the length of days from Thanksgiving to New Year's but *why* became very important to me.

It's incredibly easy to get caught up in the custom or etiquette of a certain behavior. We do certain things because, well, that's how we've always done them. When we take the time to dig a bit deeper and unearth the hidden meaning and significance of the things we feed ourselves, decorate our homes with, and gift to one another, the holidays and traditions take on such heightened significance, such deeper resonance. Now we don't just do them, we know *why* we're doing them.

In October 2010, I became a parent. That first holiday season, our son, Huxley, was so tiny and we were so sleep deprived and just trying to just keep our heads above water that the season sort of went by in a flash. The second year, though, just after he'd turned one, we were much more on our game when December rolled around. With each year he gets older, we're able to tell him just a little bit more about why we decorate an evergreen tree, or bake Stöllen, or put out luminaries, or exchange simple gifts with our loved ones this time of year. His enthusiasm is infectious, and we find ourselves getting more excited about taking him to a gingerbread house display or to hear carolers than I'd have ever thought possible.

As this time of dark days comes to a close, consider throwing a gathering of your own that acknowledges the meaning behind the edible and visual elements of the season. We held this party in our home, right around the winter solstice. Guests arrived around dusk, as the light began to cast a magical glow across the barren landscape. Everyone came dressed to the nines, with cocktail dresses, fedoras, and even bowties all accounted for. Before we ate, we gathered around the feasting table, and I shared a bit of the meaning associated with some of the flavors and sights of the season. My guests' faces lit up by candlelight, their lovingly prepared dishes spread out in front of us, a sense of wonder and awe and love permeated our evening. It was glorious.

Soon the light will return. The barrenness of winter will give way to the vigor and greenery of spring, and the days will be long and bright. Until then, this gathering is a lovely way to light up the night and imbue the chill of winter with a hefty dose of warmth.

SETTING THE SCENE

The vibe of this gathering is perhaps a bit more reverential, a bit quieter than some of the others. Merriment will certainly be had, and children are most definitely welcome, but cultivating a sort of specialness to the occasion helps to set the right tone.

CREATE A SACRED SPACE: For me, this gathering feels a bit sacred, so I like to craft a visible environment that speaks to that. In an attempt to convey the proper tone, I often host this gathering around twilight. I also put out lots of candles, dim the lights, and burn pine, cypress, juniper, or frankincense-scented incense throughout the event.

DRESS UP THE SEASON: When I throw this gathering, I like to make it a bit fancy and ask guests to don some cocktail finery. From dresses to kilts, bowties to heels, invite guests to have fun dressing up in their favorite party attire.

INCLUDE WINTER BOTANICALS: In advance of the event, ask guests to gather up greenery or other winter botanicals. Pinecones, berries, greenery, mushrooms, branches—any available wintertime botanical element is welcome. They don't necessarily need to bring a large amount, just bits of this and that to decorate the table with. As they arrive, have them place their botanicals artfully onto the table. Varying heights would be fun too, so consider placing a big branch or wood stump on the table for hanging or placing other botanicals on.

So many wonderful memories surround the holiday season. From much-loved cookies baked every year to colorful gifts under the tree, from snowball fights to spiked glasses of eggnog, everyone has some fun holiday recollection that's stayed with them for years. Once guests have settled in with food and drink, gather everyone around and ask if anyone cares to share some family traditions or experiences they fondly associate with the season. From heartwarming to hilarious, the holidays are rife with memorable events.

CUSTOMIZED CANDLES

YOU WILL NEED

- Craft paper or newspaper
- Pillar candles (1 per guest, in any height)
- Hammer or rubber mallet (or several, if available)
- Mini cookie cutters (letters, numbers, shapes, and holiday motifs will all work)
- Wire brush

So many cultures place strong significance on light and sun during the holiday season. From the Yule log to the Hanukkah menorah, from Christmas tree lights to the Kwanzaa kinara, fire and light are integral to seasonal celebrations, as this time of year heralds the end of darkness and a return to longer, brighter days. To honor that, craft customized pillar candles with your guests. Ask each of them to bring a pillar candle (or one per household in attendance) to decorate together. By gently tapping a wire brush into the candle to form a decorative motif, or pressing mini cookie cutters into the candle's side with a rubber mallet to form words, numbers, or images, guests can create a signature look for their candle. Later, at home, when that candle shines, it'll both light up the night and serve as a glowing reminder of the good times shared together at this gathering.

Set all of the supplies out on a table covered in newspaper. Have guests choose a design of their liking, using letters, numbers, images, or motifs from the miniature

BOTANICAL AND EDIBLE SIGNIFICANCE

From evergreens to cinnamon, the sights, sounds, and flavors of the holiday season are laced with meaning. Here's a sample:

· Bells: Believed to drive away winter demons hiding in the shadows of cold winter nights.
· Candles: Since fire melts winter's chill, it was thought to encourage the sun to shine and ward off evil spirits.
· Chocolate: Considered a wellspring of life.
· Evergreens: Believed to have power over death and destruction because their color never fades.
· Ornaments: Initially, fruits, nuts, cookies, candies, and flowers were used as adornments and represented offerings to thank the tree for its spirit; these items also symbolized the abundance that would return when the sun again shed its warmth.
· Pomegranates, oranges, lemons, and apples: All were emblematic of fertility.
· Poppy seeds: Representative of love and purported to ward off witches, demons, and nightmares.
· Rosemary: Symbolic of faithfulness and constancy.
· Spices (including anise seed, cinnamon, cloves, ginger, nutmeg, pepper, and star anise): Lauded for their alleged aphrodisiac properties.

cookie cutters. Holding the cookie cutter steady with one hand, gently hammer or pound it into the candlewax. It's helpful to roll the candle slightly during this process, so that the cutter makes even indentations in the wax. Alternatively, gently push a wire brush into the candle to fashion a crosshatch motif.

Smoked foods, spicy foods, long-simmered stews, citrus, evergreen herbs—anything that references heat and warmth and sunlight is the order of day at this gathering. Spices, slow-cooked meats, and roasted and braised vegetables are all welcome here. And, naturally, sweets and treats and baked goods and their kin have a very special place at the holiday table, as their enlivening flavors excite the taste buds while invigorating the spirit. I like to make appetizer-size portions for this party, so that everyone can best mix, mingle, and nosh throughout the evening. Ask guests to bring several dozen of whatever appetizer they prefer, coordinating in advance who is bringing what so as to best round out the meal.

MENU SUGGESTIONS

Sun Coins*, Sugarplums*, Wild Rice–Stuffed Mushrooms*, Wassail*,
Phyllo Cups with Leeks and Apples, Warm Chèvre with Cranberries and Pecans,
Roasted Salted Figs, Greens and Corncakes, Herbed Meatballs,
Mincemeat Mini Pies, Bûche de Noël with Meringue Mushrooms,
Pine Nut and Anise Seed Cookies, Hot Buttered Rum, Eggnog Martinis

SUN COINS

I love the idea of a savory cookie. It's not a cracker, but it's not quite a cookie either. These shortbread rounds are scented with curry powder, turmeric, hot pepper flakes, and golden raisins, all subtle, tasty references to sunlight, heat, and warmth. They are best eaten with a bold cocktail, stout beer, or robust glass of red wine, and every bite will remind you of the sunny days that winter will eventually give way to.

Makes 3 dozen

TO MAKE

In an electric mixer, beat the butter until light and fluffy. Add the sugar, curry powder, turmeric, salt and hot pepper flakes. Beat until fully combined, stopping to scrape down the beater and sides of the mixing bowl with a spatula as needed. Beat in the flour in 1-cup increments, stopping to scrape down the beater and sides of the bowl between additions. Stir in the raisins.

YOU WILL NEED

- 1 cup (2 sticks) unsalted butter, at room temperature
- 1 tablespoon sugar
- 2 teaspoons curry powder
- 1 teaspoon ground turmeric
- 1 teaspoon sea salt
- ½ teaspoon hot pepper flakes
- 2 cups all-purpose flour
- ¼ cup golden raisins

Divide the dough into 2 equal portions. On a clean countertop or cutting board, form each portion of dough into a log roughly 1½ inches wide and 7 to 8 inches long. Transfer the logs to baking parchment or wax paper (wrapping each log separately). Chill in the refrigerator until firm, at least 1 hour.

Preheat the oven to 300°F. Remove the dough logs from the refrigerator. Cut each log into ¼-inch-thick slices. You should be able to get about 18 slices per log. Bake on 2 cookie sheets for 25 minutes, rotating halfway, until the cookies begin to firm up and become fragrant.

Cool for at least 15 minutes before serving. Store in a lidded container for up to 1 to 2 months.

SUGARPLUMS

These balls of dried fruit, nuts, and spices have been a part of wintertime celebrations since long before Tchaikovsky's ballet or a certain much-loved Christmas poem. Walnuts and figs were associated with fertility, while oranges and other citrus referred to the return of the sun marked by the winter solstice. Toss in a bit of rosemary, emblematic of remembrance, and spices for protection and love, and don't be surprised if visions of these sweet morsels should dance in your head!

Makes 4 dozen

TO MAKE

Preheat the oven to 250°F. Spread the walnut pieces on a small baking pan. Toast for 5 to 6 minutes, until fragrant and just slightly browned. Set aside to cool.

Place the cooled walnut pieces and the remaining ingredients except the granulated sugar in a food processor. Begin with several pulsing bursts to break down the fruit pieces and nuts.

After the mixture begins to come together, leave the food processor to blend the ingredients fully. Depending on your machine, this should take between 2 and 4 minutes. Transfer the mixture from the food processor to a mixing bowl.

Roll about 1 tablespoon of the mixture into a ball, and then roll the ball in the granulated sugar. Repeat until the mixture has all been formed into balls.

YOU WILL NEED

- 1 cup walnut pieces
- 1 cup chopped dried figs
- 1 cup chopped dried apricots
- 1 cup chopped pitted prunes
- Zest of 1 orange
- 2 tablespoons fresh rosemary, chopped
- 1 teaspoon ground nutmeg
- 1 teaspoon ground cinnamon
- 1 teaspoon medium-grind black pepper
- ¾ teaspoon sea salt
- ½ teaspoon ground allspice
- 3 tablespoons orange liqueur (such as Cointreau or Grand Marnier) or orange juice
- Granulated sugar for rolling the balls in

Serve at room temperature. Store the sugarplum balls in between layers of baking parchment inside a lidded container. They will keep in the refrigerator for up to 1 month.

WILD RICE—STUFFED MUSHROOMS

Mushrooms have a long and storied association with winter. Ancient Lapland shamans used to eat toadstools and go on metaphysical flights throughout the universe. That's why Santa Claus wears red and white and is able to hit up so many homes in one night! While toadstools (fly agaric) are themselves poisonous, cremini or button mushrooms aren't. Stuffed with wild rice, blue cheese, sun-dried tomatoes, and rosemary, these bite-size morsels will take you away on their own flights of fancy!

Makes about 3 dozen

TO MAKE

PREPARE THE WILD RICE: Place the stock or water in a medium saucepan and bring to a boil. Add the wild rice, stir, and cover with a lid. Turn heat to lowest setting and simmer gently for 45 to 50 minutes, until the rice fluffs up a bit and absorbs all of the liquid. Remove from the heat and set aside.

PREPARE THE MUSHROOM FILLING: Remove the mushroom stems from the caps. Set the caps aside and mince the stems. Heat 2 tablespoons of the olive oil in a large sauté pan. Add the garlic and the minced mushroom stems. Cook for about 10 minutes, stirring occasionally, until any liquid has cooked off. Add the rosemary and pepper and stir to fully combine. Add the wine and cook for 2 minutes. Add the cooked wild rice and the sun-dried tomatoes. Stir and cook for several more minutes, until the liquid is all absorbed. Turn the heat off and stir in the crumbled blue cheese. Cover the pan with a lid and set aside.

YOU WILL NEED

- 2 cups chicken stock or water
- ½ cup wild rice
- 2 pounds cremini or button mushrooms
- 4 tablespoons olive oil
- 3 cloves garlic, minced
- 1 tablespoon chopped fresh rosemary
- A few grinds of black pepper
- ½ cup red wine
- ½ cup oil-packed sun-dried tomatoes, minced
- 8 ounces Gorgonzola or other blue cheese, crumbled

PREPARE THE MUSHROOM CAPS: Preheat the oven to 375°F.

Place the mushroom caps on top of a rimmed baking sheet. Pour the remaining 2 tablespoons olive oil over them. Using clean hands, toss to fully incorporate the oil into the mushrooms. Turn each mushroom stem side down on the baking sheet. Roast the mushroom caps for 15 minutes.

ASSEMBLE THE STUFFED MUSHROOMS: Divide the wild rice mixture evenly among the mushrooms, stuffing each cap with a nice rounded mound. Bake for another 15 minutes at the same temperature. Remove from the oven. Cool for 10 to 15 minutes on the pan before serving.

If not serving immediately, transfer the cooled mushrooms to a lidded container and keep refrigerated for up to 3 days. When ready to serve, warm slightly in the oven before transferring to a serving platter.

WASSAIL

YOU WILL NEED

- 2 quarts fresh apple cider
- 1 cup orange juice
- 1 cup unsweetened cran-
  berry juice
- ½ cup honey
- 6 to 8 cinnamon sticks
- A handful of whole
  cloves
- Several chunks of fresh
  ginger
- Rum (optional)

Few words are a salutation, a noun, and a verb all at once. A greeting of good health, a hot beverage, and a traditional British ceremony that blesses apple trees for a fruitful harvest, *wassail* covers many bases, all of them good. The recipe I'm sharing here is from my friend Byron Ballard. As a writer, scholar, and expert on nature-based traditions and folklore, Bryon knows a good deal about all things wassail. Don't forget to wassail your trees, per her suggestion, in the last step!

Makes about 1½ quarts

TO MAKE

Combine all the ingredients except the rum in a deep pot. Simmer over the lowest setting for at least 3 hours, stirring periodically. When you feel that the flavors have all come together to your liking, remove the pot from the heat.

If desired, stir in rum in an amount to your inclination and taste preference. Don't forget to wassail your fruit trees—especially the dear apple—if you have any, by pouring the first cupful on their roots!

Cookie Exchange

From shortbread to gingersnaps, everyone has a cookie they just can't get enough of.
This party shares the load, offering cookie bounty for all!

MANY HOLIDAY BAKING TRADITIONS both exist and endure around the globe, and for good reason. During the days of snow and ice, a sweet cookie can prove the perfect antidote to the rages of the cold. Shared with friends, in a loving atmosphere, it's quite possible that the sweetness might become even sweeter. A gathering focused on cookies presents an opportunity for guests to start enjoying the sweetness of the holiday season early. Holding the exchange early in the month allows friends to mix and mingle, nibble, and chat before the madness of the season (and all of its attendant goodness too!) takes over their schedules.

I held this gathering at the home of Jen Altman, the book's photographer. We wanted to capture as much natural light as possible, and her home is considerably brighter and larger than mine. As she is a music lover, Jen had great beats playing as we all decorated, imbibed a signature cocktail for the event, and just enjoyed one another's company before the season kicked into high gear in the upcoming weeks.

I didn't grow up with a mother particularly well versed in baking. While Mom could (and still does) cook a mean pot roast, and while her chicken and dumplings were a force to be reckoned with, the terrain of cookies, cakes, pies, and their cousins was not one she opted to navigate. My interest in the wide world of flour, leavening agents, and yeast, however, couldn't possibly be satiated. Chalk it up to a persistent sweet tooth or simply an interest in having treats that weren't otherwise going to walk into the kitchen and deposit themselves in the cookie jar or onto the cake stand, my love of baking began early.

Some time ago, I came across a magazine article outlining the holiday baking traditions of Sweden. Along with recipes, the piece described a Christmas-related old wives' tale. According to the legend, if a visitor leaves your house during the holidays without enjoying some food or drink, the Christmas spirit will leave with them. To ward off the departure of holiday happiness and cheer, the Swedes have developed a litany of sweets and beverages (including many that incorporate saffron, to represent the return of the sun after the long, dark, cold winters the country is known for), baked and brewed on a variety of days during December. Any wives' tale that couples sugar and spice with everything nice is completely fine by me.

Many of the ingredients used in holiday cookie baking pay quiet homage to the season. Spices like cinnamon, cloves, nutmeg, ginger, and allspice imbue a welcome bit of heat to chilly days. Citrus adds a bit of brightness, both in flavor and color, to colorless landscapes. Chocolate's widely touted mood-elevating properties work to chase away the blues brought on by short days and long nights. There's your validation for abundant consumption of sweet treats this season—cookies don't just taste great, they're good for you too!

SETTING THE SCENE

It stands to reason that a party focused on cookies and crafting is bound to be fun. Cue up the holiday tunes, put on some festive clothes, and enjoy a sugar-fueled afternoon with your loved ones.

SILVER BELLS: For this gathering, I like to invoke a frosty winter day. To create that effect, I like to use lots of white and silver bits of décor, with a hefty measure of glassware added in (as a nod to ice!). From candles to linens, platters to glasses, pull out your frostiest decorating elements and thank the season for an opportunity to indulge.

COOKIE STANDS: Cookies displayed on a variety of levels brings their wonderfulness to new heights, quite literally! Ask guests to bring a cake stand on which to place their cookies. If they don't have a cake stand, they can simply bring any item they have on hand that could be used to elevate their platter of cookies, such as an overturned attractive bowl, a wooden box, a square basket, or even a terra-cotta planter.

HOLIDAY TUNES: If there's ever an occasion to pull out the Bing Crosby, this is it. Consider creating a playlist of beloved holiday music. You can also seek out CD collections (I've got a great two-CD collection that's in regular rotation from Thanksgiving to New Year's), or ask guests to bring along any holiday music they're particularly fond of.

BOARD GAMES

At the cookie exchanges I host, I like to include a bit of merry-making along with the noshing and the imbibing. Historically, this manifests in the form of board game playing. The silliness injects an added bit of levity to the day, and often lets the shyest of the set have their day in the sun, as it seems that board games, charades, and other party games prove time after time to free up the inner performer in us all. If it's an option, video dance games or karaoke machines would also be fantastic additions to the revelry called for by a sweet-fueled cookie exchange.

DECORATE COOKIE TINS

YOU WILL NEED:

- Scrapbooking or similar papers for decoupage
- Craft/decoupage glue
- Craft paintbrushes
- Craft paints
- Glitter, stickers, and other embellishments
- Cookie tins

Cookie tins are lovely treasures to have on hand. Not only are they ideal vessels for transporting your sugary loot back home in, they're great for gift giving, storage, or holiday décor. Ask each guest to bring a cookie tin with him or her. They can purchase new tins at large craft supply stores, or seek out older, vintage ones at thrift and antique stores. Assemble an assortment of crafting supplies like paints, brushes, and glitter, and encourage guests to trick out their tins while they're sampling cookies, sipping on eggnog, chatting with friends, and welcoming in the holiday season.

TO MAKE

Place all of the crafting materials on a large table. Encourage guests to embellish their tins however they prefer. If you're concerned about paint or marks on the table, you may want to lay down newsprint or craft paper beforehand.

ASHLEY'S TIME-HONORED TIPS FOR A TOP-NOTCH COOKIE EXCHANGE

I've thrown, and attended, my fair share of cookie exchanges. Over the years, I've developed a few tips for throwing the best exchanges possible:

1. All cookies are allowed in my exchanges, from meringues to rice cereal treats. That said, what I do love to encourage is the use of organic and local ingredients whenever possible, like free-range eggs, butter, cream, flour, and so on, that really highlight the best foods offered in the region.

2. Four dozen cookies are the amount I always ask guests to bring. Six dozen would offer more to take away, but during the holidays, that much baking could be a lot to ask of someone.

3. Bring a large lidded container for hauling away your loot. That way no plastic wrap or aluminum foil has to be used.

4. Connect guests with one another's e-mails in the event that they really dug someone's particular cookie and want the recipe to be able to make more.

5. Ask guests to RSVP and let the host know what type of cookie they're planning to bring. This helps the host curate a well-rounded offering of cookies, should there be duplicates or overlaps.

COOKING IT UP

The dark, cold days of winter call for a hefty dose of sweetness with which to temper them. Cookie exchanges are the perfect solution to amassing a plethora of sweet treats without doing all of the work alone. While guests are certainly welcome to bring any cookie they'd like, a variety of options is always nice. To that end, ask

guests to give you a heads-up on what they might be bringing, so as to best have a well-rounded offering of spice, chocolate, sugar, nut, and other cookie choices.

Once everyone has arrived, placed their cookies on the table, and acquired a beverage, ask each guest to share what they brought and why. For some, their cookies may be a much-treasured family recipe, while others may have elected to try out something they read about in a magazine or discovered on a blog they love. Hearing everyone's stories, including the triumphs and travails that sometimes surround baking cookies, is oftentimes as much fun as feasting on the treats themselves!

MENU SUGGESTIONS

Candied Ginger and Black Pepper Cookies*, Rosemary and Orange Shortbread Cookies*,

Chocolate Crinkle Cookies*, Poppy Seed Rugelach,

Peanut Butter Cookies, Lavender Tea Cakes, Frosted Sugar Cookies,

Oatmeal Cranberry Cookies, Salted Chocolate Chip Cookies, Mexican Wedding Cookies,

Double Chocolate Walnut Cookies, Pfeffernusse, Almond Tuiles

CANDIED GINGER AND
BLACK PEPPER COOKIES

YOU WILL NEED

3½ cups all-purpose flour

1½ teaspoons baking soda

 ½ teaspoon sea salt

 1 teaspoon medium-grind
    black pepper

 ½ teaspoon ground allspice

 ¼ teaspoon ground cloves

 1 cup (2 sticks), unsalted
    butter, at room temperature

1½ cups light brown sugar

 1 large egg

 ¼ cup blackstrap molasses

 ¼ cup finely minced candied
    ginger

Granulated sugar for rolling
    the cookie dough balls in

What would the holidays be without a bit of earthy spice added to the mix? Here I've paired the apparent yet tempered heat shared by candied ginger and black pepper. These cookies would be lovely paired with a hot mug of spice tea, a wool blanket, and a crackling fire.

Makes 3½ dozen

TO MAKE

In a medium bowl, combine the flour, baking soda, salt, pepper, allspice, and cloves. Set aside.

Beat together the butter and brown sugar in an electric mixer until the blend becomes pale and fluffy. Scrape down the sides of the bowl and the beater with a spatula as necessary. Add the egg and molasses. Beat until fully blended, scraping down the bowl and beaters.

Add the flour and spice mixture in 1-cup increments. Beat until everything is fully combined, 20 to 30 seconds. Add in the crystallized ginger and beat just until it is fully incorporated into the dough. Transfer the cookie dough to a lidded container. Refrigerate for 1 to 2 hours.

Preheat the oven to 350°F. Remove the dough from the refrigerator and shape it into 1-inch balls. Roll each ball in granulated sugar. Place the balls about 1 inch apart on cookie sheets lined with baking parchment or a silicone baking mat. Bake for 15 to 18 minutes, rotating the cookie sheets halfway through the baking time, until the cookies begin to crackle on top and slightly puff up. Cool the cookies completely on a wire rack, then transfer to a lidded container.

ROSEMARY AND ORANGE SHORTBREAD COOKIES

While I love all cookies, if I were backed into a corner and forced to declare my cookie preference, it would, hands down, always go to shortbread. I love the butter, the texture, the, well, everything. What's lovely about shortbread is that it's a perfect vehicle for imparting a range of flavors. Resinous rosemary and at-its-peak-of-flavor orange zest are added to the mix, resulting in a cookie that says "Happy Holidays" in every delicious bite.

Makes 2 dozen

YOU WILL NEED

2 cups all-purpose flour

½ cup sugar

½ teaspoon sea salt

1 cup (2 sticks) unsalted
   butter, cut into chunks

2 tablespoons finely
   minced fresh rosemary

Zest of 2 oranges

Pulse the flour, sugar, and salt together in a food processor. Add the butter, rosemary, and orange zest. Pulse until the mixture begins to come together and hold its shape. This will take 1 to 2 minutes, so don't worry if the mixture looks crumbly at first.

Divide the dough in half. Place one half onto a sheet of baking parchment. Shape it into a 6-inch log and roll it up in the parchment. Repeat with the second half of dough. Place both parchment-wrapped logs in the refrigerator and chill for 1 to 2 hours.

Preheat the oven to 300°F. Line 2 cookie sheets with baking parchment or silicone baking mats. Remove the dough logs from the refrigerator. Slice each log into 12 rounds, about ½ inch thick each. Bake for about 25 minutes, until the edges just begin to brown. Cool the cookies completely on a wire rack, and then transfer to a lidded container.

CHOCOLATE CRINKLE COOKIES

I grew up eating these cookies every December. To me, they are the very definition of holiday sweetness and happy memories. While the dough will become quite stiff as you're making it, the final result is a light, airy, melt-in-your-mouth chocolate cookie

YOU WILL NEED

1½ cups sugar

½ cup canola or sunflower oil

4 ounces unsweetened chocolate, melted and cooled

2 teaspoons vanilla extract

3 large eggs

2 cups all-purpose flour

2 teaspoons baking powder

½ teaspoon sea salt

Sifted powdered sugar

that marries perfectly with whatever you're drinking, from eggnog to hot chocolate to a cold, frosty glass of milk.

Makes 3 dozen

TO MAKE

Using an electric mixer set at medium speed, combine the sugar, oil, melted chocolate, and vanilla. Beat in the eggs until well combined, scraping down the sides of the bowl with a spatula as needed.

In a separate bowl, sift together the flour, baking powder, and salt. Slowly add in the flour mixture using the lowest speed setting. Mix until the flour is fully incorporated. Transfer the cookie dough to a lidded container and refrigerate for 1 to 2 hours.

Preheat the oven to 375°F. Remove the dough from the refrigerator and shape it into 1-inch balls. Roll each ball in the powdered sugar. Place the balls about 1 inch apart on cookie sheets lined with baking parchment or a silicone baking mat. Bake for 10 to 12 minutes until cookies have puffed up and appear cracked on the surface. Cool the cookies completely on a wire rack, then transfer to a lidded container.

Soup's On

Few foods comfort the body, mind, and soul like a warming bowl of soup. This party honors the many ways in which soup nourishes.

FROM THE HOTTEST TROPICAL REGIONS to the frigid tundra, from seaside villages to mountaintop communities, an international love of soup unites. Whether composed of reindeer meat or fiery chiles, wild-caught cod or harvested yams, every culture on Earth contains, at the very least, one signature soup. Come wintertime, few dishes are more immediately comforting, and physically satisfying, than a hot bowl of soup. A gathering celebrating the tradition of soup making will be remembered long after the stockpot is washed and the ladle put away.

My very first soup memory had a profound effect on me. I was five years old, a kindergartner living in Virginia Beach, Virginia. One day, as my fellow classmates and I gathered for our daily bit of story time, our teacher read to us the book *Stone Soup*. Originally a French folk tale, the story read to us that day was written by Marcia Brown. In the tale, three hungry, weary soldiers came walking into a village. Going door-to-door asking for food or a place to sleep, the soldiers are repeatedly turned away as the village's inhabitants tell them they have no food.

This wasn't at all true, as the villagers had hid their plentiful crops and foods under mattresses, in attics, and away in barns. The soldiers, sensing all was not as it appeared, engaged in a battle of wits, declaring they'll simply have to make a pot of "stone soup." Beginning with nothing more than a stone, they're able to convince the villagers to bring them a pot, some water, some vegetables, some meat, and more. Eventually, everyone sits down to a hearty meal of soup, and the soldiers are shown to the most comfortable beds in town.

The takeaway lesson from the tale, clearly, is that an abundance of joy and happiness results when we share and collaborate and help others. This is an essential skill to learn in early childhood, when our young impulses are often selfishly motivated. In an attempt at bringing the lesson to life, my teacher assigned each child an ingredient to bring to class for creating our own pot of stone soup.

I was designated the party responsible for providing a rutabaga, which sent my mother into a bit of a tailspin. Today, everything from fresh lemongrass to ginger root can easily be acquired at most grocery stores. At the time, however, items like rutabagas weren't especially easy to come by. After numerous foiled visits to markets far and near, we eventually procured the prized root vegetable. When the class convened again to make our soup, I proudly offered up my acquisition, helped to chop it, and then dropped it into the pot.

Though it was a simple soup, I've never forgotten it. Made with my peers, with items that took some effort to gather, the soup wasn't just delicious; it was nourishing, mentally and physically. In this gathering, my hope is for a similar outcome. Instead of following a recipe to the letter, I invite guests to each contribute ingredients or items for the soup and then to collaboratively cook it together.

At the gathering I hosted, we went with an Indian food theme. What guests showed up with was as much fun as creating the soup itself. With Bhangra beats playing in the background, and bindis adorning our foreheads (a fun touch I thought my friends would enjoy), my friends and I injected a much-needed dose of warmth into the cold night. As the pot simmers and winter hovers over the landscape, you and your guests will gain nourishment from one another's company, each other's contributions, and each other's collaboration, just as my guests and I did.

SETTING THE SCENE

When considering the overall feel I wanted for this party, all I could think of was the phrase "cozy and warm." So, that's exactly what I worked to create—a comfortable environment that felt like a refuge from the frost and chill.

GLOBAL EATS AND BEATS: There's more to a culture than just its cuisine. Consider playing music harkening from whichever country you're featuring at this gathering. Ask guests if they have any cuisine-specific CDs to bring along, or tune in to a streaming channel on the Internet, such as Pandora.

SOUP BOWLS: Since the overarching theme of this gathering is collaboration, ask guests to bring soup bowls or mugs. Stacked together, in all of their mismatched glory, the vessels will serve as a silent testament to the beauty found in diversity and the ability of shared efforts to achieve beautiful outcomes.

TELLING TEXTILES: Incorporating table linens suited to the country you're focusing on is another way to inject its culture into your gathering. If possible, consider using prints or colors often associated with your given country in your décor.

DIVIDE AND CONQUER: Once everyone arrives, decide who will perform the various tasks involved in creating a pot of soup. There's chopping, seasoning, and stirring to be done, so ask guests to volunteer their preference or draw numbers to divvy up the work.

YOU WILL NEED

- One 1-pint jar per guest
- Jar labels
- 3 to 4 varieties of dry beans, such as: chickpeas, red lentils, green lentils, brown lentils, split peas, black-eyed peas, kidney beans, navy beans, black beans, pinto beans, cannellini beans, or heirloom varieties, such as scarlet or purple runner beans
- 4 to 5 dried flavorings, such as: dried onion pieces, onion powder, garlic salt, hot pepper flakes, curry powder, ground cumin, chili powder, dried chives, dried thyme, dried oregano, dried marjoram, ground black pepper, dried basil, dried parsley, and bay leaves

COLLECTIVE MEMORIES

Everyone has a soup memory to share. Whether it's Grandma's chicken noodle soup, or a friend's soul-satisfying minestrone, each of us has experienced a soup memory not soon forgotten. When giving guests advance details of the gathering, ask them to begin considering a memorable soup experience. Even if it's a pot of bean soup, lovingly tended to for hours only to be dropped on the floor when carried to the table, all memories are welcome.

MAKE SOUP MIX JARS

An at-the-ready dry soup mix is a balm to the soul of winter-weary cooks. Once your guests have put their collaboratively created pot of soup on to cook, have them gather around a table and make soup mixes. Ask each guest or family to bring a pint-size glass jar with them, along with

several cups of dried beans and a bit of seasoning from the list of suggestions below. Communicate in advance to know who's bringing what to avoid duplications.

TO MAKE

Have guests decoratively layer the beans and seasonings to their liking. Each person's jar will then have a unique flavor profile, customized just to his or her flavor preferences. On the jar labels, have each guest write the following: "Add 3 to 4 quarts of broth and cook over medium-high heat until the beans are tender and the soup is fragrant. Add salt to taste."

For this gathering, I'm deviating a bit from previous parties. Here the soup recipes are created on the spot by the guests. Select a theme or style of soup, then pass around a list of suggested ingredients in advance of the get-together and see who would like to bring what. If guests would like, they may also bring an accompaniment or side dish relevant to the featured cuisine, such as naan to pair with an Indian-inspired soup, or focaccia for an Italian soup. This is the place for imaginations to reign and creativity to flourish!

MENU SUGGESTIONS

See the ingredient suggestions within each section below.

THE FLAVORS OF INDIA: Garam Masala*, Naan, Mango Lassi, Carrot Halwa

THE FLAVORS OF ITALY: Italian Soup Croutons*, Focaccia, Chianti, Tiramisu

THE FLAVORS OF MOROCCO: Ras el Hanout*, Khobz (Moroccan Bread), Green Tea with Mint, Stuffed Dates

SOUP-MAKING SECRETS

While every pot of soup has its own unique spin (even more so when collectively cooked), there are several steps you can take toward making whatever's in your pot truly delicious. Here are several tips I've learned in my many years of soup making that'll have everyone hungrily requesting "more, please!"

· *Broth is best.* In a pinch, water will work as a means of extending your soup, but the depth of flavors afforded by broth take a soup from so-so to stellar. Depending on the soup you're making, chicken, beef, or seafood stock should all be considered. In mixed company, you might want to determine in advance whether any of your guests are vegetarian; if so, opt for a straight vegetable or a mushroom-based broth. Homemade or store-bought broth could be provided by the host or brought to the party by a guest as part of their contribution to the soup.

· *Beans take time.* Bear in mind that some beans take longer to cook than others. If your soup will include beans, know that the larger the bean, the greater the time you'll need to allocate to ensure they cook fully. Small beans like lentils and split peas will take considerably less time than larger beans like cannellini or kidney.

· *Wine adds flavor.* A splash or a glug of wine can help your soup develop complexity of flavor. The alcohol will cook off as the soup simmers, but the taste will remain, imparting subtle nuances that make for a more sophisticated dish.

· *Don't forget toppings.* Depending on which cuisine your soup highlights, toppings are a great way to impart texture and flavor. Croutons and fresh parsley are lovely in minestrone, while sour cream, minced cilantro, and toasted pumpkin seeds are delicious atop dal.

· *Taste before serving.* It might seem obvious, but remember to taste your soup one last time before serving it. This is your final opportunity to balance the flavor with a pinch of salt or squeeze of lemon, should you find the soup needs it.

THE FLAVORS OF INDIA

Think of the dals and soups of India here. Your group won't be making a traditional Indian soup, so feel free to take culinary liberties!

INGREDIENT SUGGESTIONS:

Basmati rice

Black pepper

Cardamom

Carrots

Cauliflower

Chickpeas

Chiles

Cilantro

Cloves (whole)

Coconut

Coriander

Cumin

Curry Powder

Eggplant

Fenugreek

Garlic

Ghee

Ginger

Lamb

Lentils

Mung beans

Mustard seeds

Peas

Potatoes

Pumpkin

Spinach

Tomatoes

Turmeric

Yams

Yogurt

GARAM MASALA

This traditional spice blend can be found across the kitchens of Northern India. A bit of it goes a long way toward rendering a soup with an Indian soul.

TO MAKE

Place the coriander seeds, fennel seeds, mustard seeds, cardamom seeds, cloves, bay leaf, and cinnamon in a heavy-bottom pan such as a cast-iron skillet. Dry toast the seeds over low heat for 7 to 8 minutes, stirring occasionally, until fragrant and slightly browned. Remove the pan from heat and transfer the seeds to a small bowl. Cool for about 5 minutes.

Using a coffee grinder, food processor, or mortar and pestle, grind the seeds to a powder. Place a fine sieve over a small bowl. Transfer the ground spices to the sieve. Shake it gently to release the powder to the bowl below. Discard or compost any solids.

Add the hot pepper flakes and nutmeg to the bowl and stir to fully combine. Label and store in a lidded container out of direct sunlight. Use within 6 months.

YOU WILL NEED

1½ tablespoons coriander seeds

½ tablespoon fennel seeds

2 teaspoons brown mustard seeds

2 teaspoons cardamom seeds (from several green cardamom pods)

1 teaspoon whole cloves

1 bay leaf

Half of a 2-inch cinnamon stick

½ teaspoon hot pepper flakes

½ teaspoon freshly grated nutmeg

THE FLAVORS OF ITALY

A fragrant, hearty minestrone could be your point of inspiration here. Imagine a lush Italian garden, and fire up the stove!

INGREDIENT SUGGESTIONS:

Anchovies	Garlic	Pork
Arborio rice	Lemons	Prosciutto
Artichokes	Marjoram	Romano cheese
Bacon	Nutmeg	Rosemary
Balsamic vinegar	Olives	Sage
Basil	Olive oil	Spinach
Cabbage	Onions	Split green peas
Cannellini beans	Oranges and orange zest	Thyme
Capers	Oregano	Tomatoes
Celery	Parmesan cheese	Wine
Fennel	Parsley	Zucchini
Fish	Pasta	

ITALIAN SOUP CROUTONS

While often considered a salad topping, croutons make a delicious addition to soups. Place one of these across individual bowls of soup and sigh in hearty contentment.

YOU WILL NEED

⅓ cup olive oil

2 cloves garlic, peeled and smashed

1 full-size baguette, cut into ⅓-inch slices

¼ cup grated Parmesan cheese

Freshly ground black pepper or hot pepper flakes to taste

TO MAKE

Preheat the oven to 350°F. Heat the olive oil in a small saucepan over low heat. Add the smashed garlic to the pan and sauté for about 5 minutes, stirring occasionally, until golden brown. Remove the pieces of garlic from the oil and compost or discard. Toss the olive oil with the bread slices in a baking pan, coating each slice evenly.

Place in the oven and bake for 10 minutes. Remove the baking pan from the oven, turn each of the slices over, and cook for 5 more minutes. Remove the baking pan from the oven once more. Sprinkle the cheese evenly over the crouton slices. Add some black pepper or hot pepper flakes. Return to the oven and bake for 4 more minutes, until the cheese begins to melt.

North African cuisine is both sweet and savory. Think of the hearty tagines and stews of the region as you create a Moroccan-inspired soup.

INGREDIENT SUGGESTIONS:

Almonds	Eggplant	Mint
Anise seed	Eggs	Pine nuts
Apricots (dried)	Figs	Pistachios
Beef	Flower waters (such as	Preserved lemons
Chicken	orange or rose)	Prunes
Cinnamon	Ginger	Rabbit
Couscous	Harissa	Raisins
Cumin	Honey	Saffron
Dates		

RAS EL HANOUT

A central component of Moroccan cuisine, this spice blend is Arabic for "top of the shop." Accordingly, it refers to a mixture of the best spices a person is able to obtain. Mixes vary widely, sometimes containing more than a dozen or more spices. Add a bit of this to your Moroccan-inspired soup and find yourself transported to the land of camels, palm trees, and souks.

TO MAKE

Place the coriander seeds, cumin seeds, cardamom seeds, fennel seeds, and black peppercorns in a heavy-bottom pan such as a cast-iron skillet. Dry toast over low heat for 7 to 8 minutes, stirring occasionally, until fragrant and slightly browned.

Remove the pan from heat and transfer the seeds to a small bowl. Cool for about 5 minutes.

Using a coffee grinder, food processor, or mortar and pestle, grind to a powder. Place a fine sieve over a small bowl. Transfer the ground spices to the sieve. Shake it gently to release the powder to the bowl below. Discard or compost any solids.

Add the remaining spices and the salt to the bowl. Stir to fully combine. Label and store in a lidded container out of direct sunlight. Use within 6 months.

YOU WILL NEED

2 teaspoons coriander seeds

2 teaspoons cumin seeds

1 teaspoon cardamom seeds (from several green cardamom pods)

1 teaspoon fennel seeds

1 teaspoon black peppercorns

1 teaspoon ground turmeric

1 teaspoon ground cinnamon

1 teaspoon smoked paprika

1 teaspoon ground ginger

½ teaspoon ground cloves

½ teaspoon ground allspice

½ teaspoon sea salt

Heartwarming

In my opinion, the ideal midwinter pick-me-up includes three things: warming foods and beverages, a hot fire, and the easy companionship of friends and family. This gathering incorporates all of those elements and more, warming up the chilliest days of the season.

WHEN THE GRAY SKIES, barren branches, and whipping winds of winter have taken their toll, a warming party is just what's needed. Each year, come midwinter, I'm ready for a reset, a respite, and a retreat. Comforting foods, hot fires, candlelight, and the company of loved ones are an ideal means of warming body and soul alike. Banish the cold with a gathering focusing on the best parts of the season—the food, the fire, and the faces of friends and family.

One of my favorite aspects of the colder months is all of the lovely creature comforts we get to indulge in. Wool blankets, flannel sheets, ladles of hot soup, hunks of crusty bread, good books read in cozy pajamas on the couch. The darkness of winter forces us, and many of the creatures we share this soil with, inside, underground, and under cover. It's easy to feel sullen when the days are short, the air is frigid, the ground is bare, and the land is still. The festivities, decorations, and general merriment of the holidays have passed, but there's still plenty of ice and snow and frost to come.

There's an interesting correlation between two February celebrations, Valentine's Day and the Celtic first day of spring, Imbolc. A priest condemned to death by the

Roman emperor Claudius II, Valentine was canonized as the patron saint of love for his attempts at aiding Christians under persecution by the emperor. Helping Christians was considered a crime, and Valentine was imprisoned and later beheaded for his gestures. Imbolc, alternatively, celebrates the return of spring. In the Irish climate, the signs of spring are evidenced in February. This ancient rite honors Brigid, a goddess revered for her gifts of poetry, healing, and metalsmithing.

Though they stem from different traditions, both holidays honor the spirit of love and rebirth and fire. These qualities are absolutely essential when the frosty grip of the season can make things feel stuck and rigid and hardened. Remembering the things to come is imperative now more than ever. Actively cultivating warmth inside of our homes, in our relationships, and inside our hearts is key to getting us through the dark days.

One February in my mid-twenties, I found myself on the receiving end of a long-term relationship breakup. Tired of feeling sorry for myself, I decided to kill sorrow with love, and invited several friends over. We brewed up a pot of hot chocolate, made a batch of heart-shaped sugar cookies, and set about decorating them with festive icings, toppings, and messages of love. Then we shared the cookies with each other and capped off the day with an impromptu dance party in my living room. Though the weather outside was frightful, that Valentine's Day we warmed ourselves right up, with sugar, libations, and lots of love.

I held this gathering one weekend in early February. Seven lovely lady friends and I ate heartily, basked in the warmth of one another's radiant company, and, yes, got down to dancing. The heart needs some cardio to work strong, of course, and a bit of hip-hop beats in midwinter are an ideal catalyst to get your blood pumping. As you gather with your nearest and dearest, bear in mind the transient nature of things. Ice melts, branches bud anew, days lengthen. Through the flicker of firelight, remember the story of the Phoenix, rising from the ashes, renewed, restored, and ready to live.

At its core, this gathering is all about love. While the gathering's focus needn't be romantic, it should take place with loved ones you feel especially comfortable around.

WOOL THROWS: Since this gathering is all about comfort and warmth and love,

cozy blankets are the order of the day! Ask guests to bring a warm blanket with them (if they happen to be red or plaid or red and plaid, all the better!).

GATHER AROUND A FLAME: If your location has a fireplace or woodstove indoors, gather around it, nestled down on cozy pillows. If you're hosting an outdoor gathering around a fire pit or bonfire, bundle up in warm coats, gloves, and hats, and drape the blankets over everyone's shoulders. If a fireplace or fire pit isn't available, ask your guests to bring a small red candle. Set the candles on the mantle indoors or in sturdy glass jars or luminary bags weighted down with sand outdoors.

A LOVELY DAY: Compiling a playlist of heartwarming, loving songs would be a welcome complement to the gathering. Poll your guests in advance, asking for the tunes that warm their hearts the most, then create a soundtrack for the gathering based around their suggestions. You could post the playlist on a shared site such as Spotify for everyone to enjoy long after the day has passed.

SHARING THE EXPERIENCE
HEARTWARMING TALES

The goal of this gathering is to warm winter-weary bodies and minds. Along with the food, crafts, décor, and camaraderie, ask guests to share stories or anecdotes of things they've experienced, heard of, or read about that warmed their hearts. I always love stories about random acts of kindness, even if it's a simple one, like paying for the coffee of the person in line behind you or leaving flowers on someone's front steps. The host can mention this activity in the invitation, so that guests have time to consider what they'd like to share.

MAKE MUSTARD BATH POWDER

An absolute salvation in winter, a mustard bath is a traditional English remedy used in the treatment of colds, stress, fatigued and achy muscles, fever, and congestion.

Relief is offered from mustard's purported abilities to stimulate sweat glands and increase circulation in the body, pulling out impurities and toxins in the process. Adding baking soda and stimulating essential oils to the mustard yields a product that is as detoxifying as it is invigorating.

Whipping up a batch of mustard powder for guests to take home is a great way of keeping hearts and bodies warm, long after the gathering has passed. The host can provide all of the ingredients or individual guests can be assigned specific ingredients, to bring with them. Once prepared, the powder can be placed in waxed paper bags provided by the host or small glass jars, which each guest could bring along. To increase the quantity, simply double, triple, or quadruple the ingredients as necessary.

Makes enough for 4 baths

YOU WILL NEED

1 cup baking soda

¼ cup mustard powder

6 drops wintergreen essential oil

6 drops rosemary essential oil

6 drops eucalyptus essential oil

Using a whisk, combine all the ingredients in a lidded container. When ready to use, add about ¼ cup of powder to a running bath. Swish the water around with your hands to disperse it. Soak for as long as you are comfortable, topping off with warmer water as needed.

COOKING IT UP

Heartwarming foods are those that warm and invigorate both the body and soul. Think hearty, robust dishes like pot roast and macaroni and cheese, ricotta-spinach soufflés, and anything with ginger. Chocolate is welcome too, as its properties have been known to chase the blues far, far away. Citrus is at its peak during winter months, and its bright, fresh notes and bold hues would be welcome at any table.

MENU SUGGESTIONS

Warming Steak and Bourbon Cottage Pie*, Chocolate Orange Gingerbread*,
Decadent Hot Chocolate*, Winter Greens and Gruyère Hand Pies, Spiced Meat Potpie,
Warm Beet and Orange Salad, Corned Beef and Cabbage, Curried Winter Squash Soup,
Cheddar Biscuits, Zesty Three-Bean Chili, Mini Cheese-Stuffed Potatoes,
Apple Cider Hot Toddies, Fudgy Chocolate Stout Brownies

WARMING STEAK AND BOURBON COTTAGE PIE

I had my first cottage pie years ago, when I was just a child. Even then I knew it was quite possibly one of the finest, most genius dishes ever conceived. Flaky, buttery pastry cradles a rich mushroom, carrot, steak, and brandy filling, while a creamy potato topping protects from above. On a cold winter's night, this is the food you want warming you.

Serves 8 to 10

YOU WILL NEED

FOR THE PIECRUST

1¼ cups all-purpose flour

¾ teaspoon sea salt

½ cup (1 stick) butter, chilled and cubed

⅔ cup ice water

FOR THE MEAT FILLING

2 tablespoons neutral-flavored oil, such as peanut

2 pounds inexpensive steak, such as London broil

1 tablespoon unsalted butter

1 medium white onion, diced

3 carrots, diced

2 ounces dried porcini mushrooms, rehydrated in hot water

3 cloves garlic, minced

2 tablespoons all-purpose flour

1 cup brandy or red wine

2 tablespoons Worcestershire sauce

1 tablespoon finely chopped fresh rosemary (or 1 teaspoon dried)

1 teaspoon sea salt

Several grinds of black pepper

FOR THE POTATO TOPPING

4 pounds medium starchy potatoes, peeled and quartered, with some skin left on

½ cup (1 stick) butter, at room temperature

1 cup heavy cream

½ teaspoon sea salt

Several grinds of black pepper

TO MAKE

PREPARE THE PIECRUST: Mix the flour and salt together in a medium-large bowl. Using a pastry cutter or 2 forks, incorporate the butter until the mixture resembles a coarse meal (you should still have rather large bits of butter when you're done). Slowly drizzle in the ice water. Stir with a mixing spoon until the dough starts to clump.

Transfer the dough onto a floured work surface and fold it together into itself using your hands. The dough should come together easily but should not feel overly sticky. Shape it into a flattened disk. Wrap in cellophane or place in a lidded container and refrigerate for at least 1 hour.

Remove the dough dish from the refrigerator. Roll out the dough on a lightly floured surface into a 9 × 13-inch rectangle. Transfer the pastry dough to a 9 x 13-inch glass, ceramic, or metal baking pan. Place the pan in the refrigerator to chill while preparing the filling.

PREPARE THE MEAT FILLING: Heat a heavy-bottom pan over high heat. Add the oil, then sear the steak for several minutes on each side until browned. Remove the meat from the pan and set aside. Reduce the heat to medium. Melt the butter in the pan, then add the onion and carrots. Cook for 10 to 12 minutes, until the onions are translucent and the vegetables are all a bit brown around the edges. Add the rehydrated mushrooms and stir. Add the garlic and cook for 3 to 5 more minutes.

Stir in the flour and cook for 1 to 2 minutes. Add the brandy, Worcestershire sauce, rosemary, salt, and pepper. Cook for about 5 minutes, until the liquid has evaporated. Cut the steak across the grain into small bite-size pieces. Stir the steak into the carrots and onions. Cook for 2 minutes, then remove from the heat.

PREPARE THE POTATOES: Bring a large pot of water to a boil. Add the potatoes and cook for about 20 minutes, until fork tender. Remove the potatoes from heat and drain in a colander. Mash the butter into the potatoes. Add the cream and mash a bit more (it should still be just a little chunky). Stir in the salt and pepper.

ASSEMBLE THE PIE: Preheat the oven to 400°F.

Remove the pan containing the pie dough from the refrigerator.

Spread the steak filling evenly across the bottom of the pan. Spread the potato topping evenly across the meat. Bake for 35 to 40 minutes, until the crust and potato topping both turn golden brown. Cool for at least 20 to 30 minutes before serving.

CHOCOLATE ORANGE GINGERBREAD

++++++++++++++++++++++++++++++++

YOU WILL NEED

1½ cups all-purpose flour

⅓ cup dark cocoa powder

1 teaspoon sea salt

1 teaspoon baking soda

½ teaspoon ground ginger

½ teaspoon ground cinna-
mon

¼ teaspoon ground cloves

½ cup (1 stick) unsalted butter, at room temperature,
plus extra for greasing the
pan

¾ cup light brown sugar

1 large egg

⅔ cup blackstrap molasses

¾ cup boiling water

¼ cup minced crystallized
ginger

Zest of 2 medium
oranges

Powdered sugar to deco-
rate (optional)

++++++++++++++++++++++++++++++++

What could be more warming than zesty ginger-bread? Add cocoa powder and orange zest to a hearty doze of crystallized ginger and you've got a trifecta of heat-stimulating deliciousness. A hearty dollop of whipped cream would do wonders to ward off winter's chill too!

Makes 6 to 8 slices

TO MAKE

Preheat the oven to 350°F. Lightly butter a 9-inch round cake pan. Set aside.

In a medium bowl, sift together the flour, cocoa powder, salt, baking soda, ground ginger, cinnamon, and cloves. Set aside. Using an electric mixer, beat the butter and brown sugar together at medium speed until the butter becomes pale and the mixture turns light and fluffy, 2 to 3 minutes. Add the egg and molasses and beat until well combined. Scrape down the sides of the bowl and the beaters.

On low speed, beat in half of the flour mixture. Scrape down the sides of the bowl with a spatula. Beat in the boiling water and scrape down the bowl. Add the remaining half of the flour mixture and beat until fully blended. Scrape down the bowl. Still on low speed, beat in the crystallized ginger pieces and orange zest just until combined with the cake batter.

Transfer the batter to the prepared cake pan. Smooth out the surface of the cake

with an offset spatula. Bake for 35 to 40 minutes, until the center of the cake has set. Cool on a wire rack for at least 30 minutes before serving. If desired, sprinkle powdered sugar decoratively over the surface of the gingerbread.

DECADENT HOT CHOCOLATE

When I was on my honeymoon, my husband and I had the pleasure of enjoying the thick, rich hot chocolate offered at Angelina's in Paris. This is my homage to that delightful experience. Though its tastiness may tempt you to imbibe furiously, this is a sipping chocolate, so take your time, savoring every exquisite sip.

Makes 3 cups

YOU WILL NEED

- 3 cups whole milk
- 4 tablespoons good-quality cocoa powder
- 2½ ounces good-quality baking chocolate
- 3 tablespoons sugar
- 1 tablespoon honey

OPTIONAL ADD-INS

- ¼ cup coffee-flavored liqueur, such as Kahlúa
- Pinch of freshly grated nutmeg
- Pinch of ground cinnamon
- ¼ teaspoon orange extract
- Marshmallows (optional)

TO MAKE

Warm the milk in a medium saucepan over medium-low heat. Add the remaining ingredients (add the coffee liqueur just before serving if you want to retain some of the alcohol). Whisk to combine.

Continue whisking over low heat for the next 15 minutes, until the mixture is perfectly creamy and slightly reduced. Pour into individual mugs, add marshmallows, and enjoy.

Resources

BEESWAX PILLAR CANDLES

BIG DIPPER WAX WORKS

www.bigdipperwaxworks.com

CANNING EQUIPMENT (JARS, LIDS, SCREW BANDS, AND TOOLS)

LEHMAN'S

www.lehmans.com

CLOTH PRODUCE BAGS

PEARLY BIRDS

www.etsy.com/shop/PearlyBirds

COOKIE CUTTERS (MINI LETTERS, NUMBERS, AND SHAPES)

ATECO

www.atecousa.com

COOKIE TINS

INDEPENDENT CAN COMPANY

www.cookietins.us

CRAFT ENVELOPES (MINI)

PAPER FISH STUDIO PAPERGOODS

www.etsy.com/shop/pfspapergoods

ESSENTIAL OILS

SIMPLERS BOTANICALS

www.shopsimplers.com

FLORACOPEIA

www.floracopeia.com

FLORAL SUPPLIES (BOUILLON WIRE, CORSAGE PINS)

SAVE ON CRAFTS

www.save-on-crafts.com

GIFT TAGS (OKRA STAMPS)

PAPER CREATIONS BY DEB

www.etsy.com/people/PaperCreationsbyDeb

HERBS (MUSTARD BATH
POWDER AND ROOT BEER)

MOUNTAIN ROSE HERBS

www.mountainroseherbs.com

JAR LABELS (DRIED SOUP MIX)

ADORE NEKO

www.etsy.com/shop/AdoreNeko

MUSLIN BAGS
(MULLING SPICES)

THAT FINAL TOUCH

www.etsy.com/people/ThatFinalTouch

PINWHEEL PAPER

PAPER SOURCE

www.paper-source.com

MICHAELS

www.michaels.com

ETSY

www.etsy.com

RUBBER STAMP
(HONEYBEE)

NORAJANE

www.etsy.com/shop/norajane

SEEDS: VEGETABLES AND
POLLINATING HERBS
AND FLOWERS

BAKER CREEK HEIRLOOM SEEDS

www.rareseeds.com

HIGH MOWING ORGANIC SEEDS

www.highmowingseeds.com

SEEDS OF CHANGE

www.seedsofchange.com

TERRITORIAL SEED COMPANY

www.territorialseed.com

SOUP MIX JARS

MIGHTY NEST

www.mightynest.com